NOT SO DUMB

NOT SO DUMB

Four Plays For Young People

John Lazarus

COACH HOUSE PRESS
TORONTO

© John Lazarus, 1993

These plays are fully protected under the copyright laws of Canada and all other countries of the Copyright Union and are subject to royalty. Changes to a script are expressly forbidden without written consent of the author. Rights to produce, film, record in whole or in part, in any medium or in any language, by any group, *amateur or professional,* are retained by the author. Interested persons are requested to apply for permission and terms to:

Patricia Ney
Christopher Banks and Associates
219 Dufferin Street, Suite 305
Toronto, Canada
M6K 1Y9

The punctuation of these plays carefully adheres to the author's instructions.

Published with the assistance of the Canada Council, the Department of Communications, the Ontario Arts Council, and the Ontario Publishing Centre.

Canadian Cataloguing in Publication Data

Lazarus, John, 1947-
 Not so dumb : four plays for young people

ISBN 0-88910-453-0

I. Title.

PS8573.A96N68 1993   C812'.54   C93-093425-3
PR9199.3.L393N68 1993

CONTENTS

Introduction *Dennis Foon*	7
Schoolyard Games	13
Not So Dumb	61
Night Light	107
Secrets	147

INTRODUCTION

During my tenure as Artistic Director of Vancouver's Green Thumb Theatre from 1985 to 1987, one of my greater pleasures was dramaturging and directing the premieres of John Lazarus's trilogy of plays for children, *Schoolyard Games, Not So Dumb* and *Night Light*. After my departure from the company I was delighted to see the characters in the trilogy continue to grow up in *Secrets*, a play that furthers John's study of the nature of friendship and that, in some ways, brings this cycle of dramas full circle.

Around 1979, when I first approached John to write a play for Green Thumb, I was surprised to learn that he'd never written a play for children. I was puzzled by this because his plays demonstrate such an affinity for the genre: playfulness, warmth, empathy, strong storytelling ability and funny, realistic dialogue. John leapt at the offer, stating that he wanted to write something that dealt with the 'jungle' of the playground that he'd witnessed his own daughters struggle with day to day. The result was *Schoolyard Games*, a deceptively simple look at the lives of three young girls which, on closer analysis, works as an examination of betrayal.

Beneath the chants, teasing and power struggles between the three girls is a terrible turbulence that the dialogue only hints at, but that the action reveals. Clearly, each of the girls is suffering inside, and though they rarely speak of their internal pain, they continually act it out on each other.

Loneliness and anger resonate through all the plays in this cycle, but in *Schoolyard Games* Eleanor's flashes of violence are, for me, terribly unsettling. She's a timebomb: that makes her scary and rather unique for a female character in the literature of theatre for the young. Her volatility enables her to control the other girls, and sets the scene for a bruising series of betrayals.

During the public premiere performance of *Schoolyard Games* at the Vancouver East Cultural Centre, Wendy Noel, who played Susan, landed badly on a jump and broke a bone in her foot, ending up in a cast. A discussion with John led to quick rewrite and rehearsal. John temporarily wrote Wendy's plaster cast into the play, making it represent yet another injury inflicted on Susan by Eleanor. Perhaps this weighed the scales a bit against poor Eleanor, but it did underline the intensity, and danger, of Eleanor's unchecked fury.

After the success of *Schoolyard Games* I was approached by the Vancouver Association for Children and Adults with Learning Disabilities which wanted to commission Green Thumb to create a play for them, promising to remain arm's-length advisors. I was intrigued by the statistic that the majority of our jails are populated by people with learning disabilities. Nevertheless, I still approached John with great trepidation for neither of us is interested in plays made to order. John took some research materials away to read in order to decide if he was interested in the commission. He returned a few days later in a creative frenzy: he had discovered that Binnie, one of the characters in *Schoolyard Games*, is a classic dyslexic!

I'm not sure whether or not John had already been contemplating the survival of the *Schoolyard Games* characters, but this new discovery secured their continued development. His determination gave him another stab at a character he loved working with, one whose layers he still wanted to unpeel.

Whereas *Schoolyard Games* concerns itself with betrayal, *Not So Dumb* flips the coin to look at loyalty. The two new characters in *Not So Dumb*, Rocky and Victor, are types so distinctively drawn that they emerge as complex, believable people. Rocky, the apparent bully, suffers from dyslexia and dysgraphia and proves to be an utterly compassionate soul. Victor, the school 'brain,' gradually reveals that his exterior also is a facade that he uses to protect himself from relentless teasing. Until John's autobiographical play, *Homework & Curtains*, appeared, Victor was the best example of the playwright's own childhood. As John confessed to us in rehearsal, he created Victor from personal experience: he too was a much maligned and isolated whiz kid. It stands to reason that John's extraordinary empathy for the 'special' child stems from his first-hand knowledge.

Empathy is at the centre of *Not So Dumb*, so it's no wonder that John was thrilled to re-introduce Binnie in this play: she's a kid whose heart and warmth saturate *Schoolyard Games*. The surface conflict of the play is between the 'brain' and the 'dummies,' with each side learning to respect the other's differences. But the play resonates because it goes beneath the surface to reveal the characters' humanity. Each suffers in isolation and their meeting allows them to express their pain and be there for each other. All these characters find out what they're finally willing to stand up for.

Not So Dumb moves the cycle a profound step forward. The kids in this play don't just gain knowledge of each other, they solve problems and thereby acquire control over what appears to be a disaster: the loss of their beloved teacher. This is a significant progression from the conclusion of *Schoolyard Games*, a play that ends with only a little understanding and a shaky truce. Without stretching the grounds of credulity very far, *Not So Dumb* demonstrates how children can gain power over their circumstances by confronting the adult in charge. In this case, the kids are lucky: the Principal listens; they aren't betrayed and they don't betray each other. It's an optimistic ending, perhaps, but certainly a worthwhile model.

Night Light further explores the use of friendship to empower. Victor, back again, learns how to overcome the bully, Farley, and to help his sister, Tara, master her fear of the dark.

Of the four plays in this volume, *Night Light*, with the introduction of the Monster, is the only one to use overt 'fantasy.' Throughout the 1980s, Green Thumb Theatre (like many other theatres for the young) eschewed fantasy in their plays out of a desire to mirror the actual lives of their audience. This trend was a stated reaction to a theatre for children that historically had been dominated by expurgated fairy tales and condescending fantasies that had little relevance to kids' lives. The aim was both political and aesthetic, and it opened up a wide range of possibilities for artists working in Theatre for Young Audiences.

John clearly has a gift for this approach, as evidenced in *Schoolyard Games,* but he often stated to me his desire to break out of realism. His use of puppets in *Not So Dumb* was a small attempt to introduce some heightened theatricality into the play, although the puppets never take on a life of their own, but remain playthings of the characters. The true theatricality of the first two plays derives from a strictly realistic base: in *Schoolyard Games,* the physical activity of the kids creates a visual feast; in *Not So Dumb,* the 'break-in' of the filing cabinet and Binnie's mirror-writing are the visual highlights. John wanted to go further than this. John's original plan was to have a clump of clothing become animate at night, terrifying Tara. In many ways, this would have been an intriguing choice because it is a universal experience: we have all watched our dirty laundry transform when the lights go off. In the end, however, he decided to have a monster inhabit Tara's chest of drawers, a monster that only she could see. In the playing it is easy to see why it's a reasonable choice: the monster can become a fully developed character with its own personality, motivations and fears. It's no small wonder that Goodge (as our actors affectionately dubbed the Monster) has such enduring appeal for young audiences: it's ugly, scary, controllable and ultimately loveable.

Night Light is the simplest of John's TYA plays and arguably the most popular. But though it may be lighthearted, it deals directly with some very troubling fears, again demonstrating the importance and power of friendship. In this play, all of the characters are transformed by what they give and what they receive.

In *Secrets,* John returns to the theme of betrayal first introduced in *Schoolyard Games,* but gives it a

INTRODUCTION

post-pubescent perspective. Susan, Binnie, Victor and Rocky are brought back as teenagers caught up in the angst of adolescent sexuality. These are appropriate characters for the task because many of their problems in the other plays surround issues of self-esteem.

In this play, John uses the device of 'asides' to allow the characters to tell the audience the secrets they're afraid to confide to their friends, creating a goldmine of amusing double entendres and painful betrayals. *Secrets* explores a number of ambiguities in relationships with enormous empathy for the characters, no matter how badly they sometimes behave. Here, once again, John points a way through confusion and pain: honesty is the ultimate test of friendship.

John's compassion informs all four of the works in this volume; his plays chart the characters' course of growth and friendship in a unique and heartfelt way. It's a journey of discovery that I hope will continue for a long, long time.

Dennis Foon
Vancouver, February 1993

SCHOOLYARD GAMES

Production History

Schoolyard Games was first produced by Green Thumb Theatre for Young People, at the Vancouver East Cultural Centre, Vancouver, on February 22, 1981, with the following cast:

ELEANOR, Anne Clark
SUSAN, Wendy Noel
BINNIE, Barbara Duncan

Directors: Dennis Foon and Jane Howard Baker
Set and Costume Designer: Randolph Nicholson

Subsequently it received a second production by Green Thumb, and productions by Chinook Theatre (Edmonton), Young People's Theatre (Toronto), Great Canadian Theatre Company (Ottawa), Actors Showcase (Winnipeg), and Grand Theatre (London, Ontario).

This Text

This script was transcribed in May 1989 from the Playwrights Union of Canada edition of November 1981. The format is different, and there are some changes in the stage directions and punctuation, but none in the actual dialogue.

Acknowledgements

My thanks to Dennis and Jane, to Anne, Wendy and Barbara, and to my daughters Naomi and Emma.

Characters
ELEANOR Ten.
SUSAN Nine.
BINNIE Eight.

ELEANOR and BINNIE are sisters and as different from each other as they can manage to be. ELEANOR is the tallest, BINNIE the shortest. ELEANOR has some skill as a gymnast.

Setting

Part of a playground. A carpeted area represents grey pavement. A jungle gym, a pair of parallel bars, a low railing. The railing is the right size so that BINNIE can wrap herself around it and do somersaults without banging her head on the ground. The jungle gym and parallel bars are useable.

The girls are usually in motion: climbing, skipping, running around, hanging from the structure in peculiar positions.

At the beginning no one is on-stage. The voices are heard from different parts of the theatre or gymnasium

SUSAN [*off*] Binnie! Binnie!
BINNIE [*off*] Whaddaya want!
SUSAN [*off*] Where's Eleanor!
BINNIE [*off*] Who cares!
ELEANOR [*off*] Susan!
SUSAN [*off*] Yeah!
BINNIE [*off*] There she is!
ELEANOR [*off*] Race you to the top of the jungle gym!

[*Enter all three, severally,* SUSAN *carrying a skipping rope. They converge on the jungle gym and clamber to the top. Much cheerful noise, ad libbing, horseplay. Then a brief pause*]

BINNIE What do we do now?
SUSAN Let's skip. I got my new rope.

[*With more noise, they clamber down and arrange to skip double Dutch. They ad lib throughout, with skipping rhymes or perhaps simple counting.* SUSAN *goes first, then* BINNIE. *As* ELEANOR *is about to jump in:*]

SUSAN Okay, you gotta beat [*whatever the highest score was*].
ELEANOR Oh, easy. [*jumps in, immediately catches ankle*

on the rope] Another turn.
SUSAN No, that was it, Eleanor, that was your turn.
ELEANOR I didn't even have a chance, Susan. I want another turn.
SUSAN You'll have a chance next time, it's mine now.
ELEANOR Your turns always go on and on.
BINNIE That's 'cause she's good.
ELEANOR It isn't fair! I want an extra turn!
BINNIE I even went longer than you did, that time.
ELEANOR Binnie—
BINNIE [*chants*] I went longer than Eleanor, I went longer than Eleanor—
ELEANOR You did not. That wasn't a real turn.
SUSAN Same rules for everybody. Come on, Eleanor. [*tries to give her the rope handle*]
ELEANOR I didn't even get to go as long as my baby sister.
BINNIE That's 'cause I'm better than you are and I'm only eight, ha ha.
ELEANOR [*advancing, fists clenched*] Binnie, just watch it!
BINNIE [*backing off*] Sorry, sorry!
SUSAN [*intervenes*] Take it easy.
ELEANOR I want another turn.

[SUSAN *hands* ELEANOR *the rope handles.* ELEANOR *and* BINNIE *begin turning the rope as* SUSAN *prepares to jump in*]

This is very unfair. Very unfair! Extremely! [*turns rope impossibly fast*]
SUSAN Heyy!

[ELEANOR *drops rope handles, sulks*]

Hey I get short turns sometimes, and I don't ask for another one.

BINNIE We should make a rule. Let's make a rule!

ELEANOR I only tripped because of your skipping rope, you know. It's your stupid skipping rope's fault.

SUSAN This is a brand new skipping rope. My dad gave it to me for my birthday. Don't call it stupid.

ELEANOR Why, is it smart? Does it have brains?

SUSAN [*amused*] No, but don't call it stupid, you'll hurt its feelings!

BINNIE [*chants*] Stupid skipping rope, stupid skipping rope!

ELEANOR Is it smarter than Binnie?

SUSAN *No ...*

ELEANOR Well, then, it's stupid!

[*All three laugh*]

BINNIE It's the stupidest skipping rope in the world!

ELEANOR Well, if it's like you it is.

BINNIE [*dances around the stage, chanting*] Stupid skipping rope stupid skipping rope stupid skipping rope ...

ELEANOR Tie her up!

[*They jump on* BINNIE, *and with much noise and to-do wrap her up in the rope.* SUSAN *and* ELEANOR *separate from her, leaving her lying on the ground chortling to herself. Brief pause*]

ELEANOR Susan, there is something wrong with your rope.

SUSAN No there isn't. Just 'cause you got tangled up, it isn't the rope's fault.

ELEANOR Susan, use your head. I'm a gymnast, right? I'm on the team and everything, right?
SUSAN [*warily*] Yeah …
ELEANOR Gymnasts do not get tangled in good ropes. I used to have a very expensive skipping rope and I never got tangled in it.
SUSAN Binnie, did you get tangled in my rope?
BINNIE Nope.
SUSAN Well.
ELEANOR Well, I'm not gonna go on arguing about it.
SUSAN Oh, it's fine.
ELEANOR Yeah, well, like I said, there's no point in arguing.

[ELEANOR *climbs away on the jungle gym. Silence.*
ELEANOR *performs gymnastics,* BINNIE *climbs thoughtfully, and* SUSAN *skips, trying the rope.* ELEANOR *watches* SUSAN *surreptitiously*]

SUSAN [*to herself, under her breath*] Fudge, fudge, tell the judge,
Momma's gonna have a baby,
Pearl, pearl, it's a girl,
Daddy's going crazy.
Wrap it up in tissue paper,
Send it up the elevator,
First—floor—*stop*—
ELEANOR I wonder when they're gonna get here. They should be here by now.
SUSAN [*having lost the rhythm*] You interrupted my skip.
ELEANOR Does anybody know what time it is?
SUSAN No.

BINNIE Time to get a watch!
SUSAN It's around four.
ELEANOR They should be here by now.
SUSAN Who?
ELEANOR Oh, just some friends of mine. We're going out.

[*Brief pause*]

SUSAN That's nice. [*skips*]
BINNIE What are you talking about?
ELEANOR Binnie's forgotten already. I told you at breakfast.
BINNIE Is it a boy?
ELEANOR Oh, Binnie, really.
BINNIE Eleanor's got a boyfriend! Eleanor's got a boyfriend!
ELEANOR No I don't! I do not, Binnie.
BINNIE Well, I think you're waiting for a boy. Who is it? Mike Grzeda?
ELEANOR No! I am not waiting for dumb Mike Grzeda. It isn't a boy.
BINNIE Who, then?
ELEANOR You want me to tell you, Susan?
BINNIE Yes! Yes! Tell us, tell us!
SUSAN No.

[*Brief pause*]

ELEANOR You sure you don't want me to tell you?
BINNIE Uh, we don't care.
ELEANOR Okay.

SCHOOLYARD GAMES

[*Sitting high on the jungle gym,* ELEANOR *turns her back to them to gaze into the distance for signs of the mysterious visitors.* BINNIE *and* SUSAN *have a flustered, whispered conversation, inaudible to us:* SUSAN *is prompting* BINNIE, *who can't remember. Suddenly* BINNIE *clues in*]

BINNIE Oh! Oh, yeah! The gymnastics tournament!

ELEANOR Whew, she remembers.

BINNIE Eleanor and her gym team are going to watch a gymnastics tournament! She's going with Mavis O'Connell and Andrea Marcus and David and Paul and Emma and, um—

ELEANOR Naomi—

BINNIE And Jo-Anne! The whole group! And Miss Larson's gonna drive them.

SUSAN *Where* you going?

ELEANOR It's for us to watch the high school gymnastics tournament. The Provincials.

BINNIE With the best gymnasts from all over the world!

ELEANOR All over the *province*, Bin, that's why it's called the *Provincials*.

BINNIE Whatever. You tell it.

ELEANOR It's the championships. Balance beam, uneven parallel bars, vaulting, tumbling, all that stuff. It's gonna go on until midnight. They're having it at the high school.

SUSAN Can I come too?

BINNIE Me too, me too! Can I come too, Eleanor?

ELEANOR Nope. This is just for those people who are going.

BINNIE Take me with you! I'll be your best friend.

ELEANOR You can't be my best friend. You're my sister.

SUSAN Eleanor?

BINNIE I'll be your best sister!

ELEANOR You're my only sister. [*aside to* SUSAN] Thank goodness.

BINNIE Very funny.

ELEANOR Anyway, Binnie, Mom wants you home by four-thirty.

BINNIE So what?

ELEANOR Oh, please, Bin, if you're not home in time we'll both get heck.

SUSAN I don't have to be home this afternoon. I could phone my father.

ELEANOR What?

SUSAN Eleanor, can I come to the gym tournament! Please.

ELEANOR It's just for the team.

SUSAN No it's not. Whatsername isn't on the team. Whatserface there. Jo-Anne.

ELEANOR Oh. [*brief pause*] Well, she's trying out.

SUSAN Whaddaya mean!

ELEANOR [*embarrassed*] I mean she's been practising a lot, and she's gonna try out for it in a few weeks.

SUSAN What about me! What do you think I been doing? All those lessons you been giving me and stuff?

ELEANOR Well, I know you're interested, but it's like—

SUSAN Whaddaya think this is! [*performs a cartwheel*] Eh?

BINNIE [*applauds*] Yay Susan!

SUSAN Yeah.

ELEANOR You're not supposed to do that without a warm-up.

SUSAN I've been doing this stuff so I can join the team! You think I'm learning this for fun? How come Jo-Anne can go with you and I can't?

ELEANOR You have to have permission from your parents.
SUSAN I could run ask my father. He wouldn't mind. He never minds when I go off somewhere.
ELEANOR Well, it has to be okay with Miss Larson.
SUSAN Well, let's ask her!
ELEANOR Miss Larson's been training Jo-Anne, she knows Jo-Anne's trying out. But she doesn't know about you. *I* been training you. I'm not really supposed to do that.
SUSAN But you been doing it right. We been doing it right.
ELEANOR I know. But she's never even met you. [*sees them, off*] There they are! [*waves*] Coming!
SUSAN Bring me over there and introduce me. We don't have to tell her you been giving me lessons. You could just ask her if I could go.

[ELEANOR *is looking at the ground*]

It wouldn't do any harm to ask, would it?
ELEANOR It costs money to go. It costs two dollars.
SUSAN So I can borrow it from you. I'll pay you back tomorrow, we aren't that poor, you know. [*pause*] How come Jo-Anne can go and I can't?
ELEANOR [*starting to leave*] I gotta go.
SUSAN [*grabbing her arm*] How come Jo-Anne's okay and I'm not!
ELEANOR Jo-Anne's eleven!
SUSAN [*pause. Lets go of* ELEANOR*'s arm*] Jo-Anne's eleven?
ELEANOR Yeah. And she's friends with all of them. And all the rest of the team are like eleven and twelve.
SUSAN So what are you doing there, Eleanor, you're ten!
ELEANOR Well—I'm tall.

SUSAN You're tall! What has that got to do with anything!
ELEANOR Susan, you're one of my best friends, and all that, but I never get to go anywhere without you hanging around. It's always you and Binnie. I want to be with somebody older instead. Or just my teammates.
SUSAN Your *teammates*.
ELEANOR It's not your fault. You can't help it if you're younger than somebody. If I have other friends, eh? Look! I'll give you another gym lesson tomorrow!
SUSAN I don't want a gym lesson tomorrow! I want to go with you now! Pleeeze?
ELEANOR [*answering an apparent call or honk from off*] I'm coming! I'll see you tomorrow. Don't forget, Binnie, home by four-thirty. [*starts to exit*]
BINNIE The hug, the hug! You forgot the hug!
ELEANOR [*coming back*] Gee, can't forget the hug.

[BINNIE *jumps onto* ELEANOR *and slides down her onto the ground, giggling.* ELEANOR *laughs*]

Creep! [*to both*] See ya!

[ELEANOR *runs off. Silence.* SUSAN *picks up her rope, drops it, sits*]

BINNIE Hey Susan, you know what I can do? Susan, watch.

[BINNIE *climbs the jungle gym, hangs upside down by her knees*]

Susan, *watch*.

[*No response*]

Susan, you better watch before I fall on my head.
SUSAN I'm watching.
BINNIE You are not.
SUSAN [*looks briefly*] There, I watched.
BINNIE Can I get down now?
SUSAN No, stay up there the rest of your life.
BINNIE Very funny. [*climbs down*] You don't have to be such a grouch, you know. [*tickles* SUSAN]
SUSAN Dooon't!
BINNIE Okay, watch this. Soooper girrrl!

[BINNIE *runs at low railing, leaps onto it, wraps herself around it, does somersault, falls dramatically on ground*]

Ta-daaah!
SUSAN Terrific. She coulda taken me, you know.
BINNIE Is that all you can say? Hey, I know, watch this. Kung fooo! [*approaches* SUSAN, *arms and legs flailing*] Hiya! Ha! Tchoo! Pah! Kow! I'm gonna make you paralyzed without hardly touching you. You wanna see me make you paralyzed without hardly touching you?
SUSAN No.
BINNIE Okay watch, I'm gonna paralyze you without hardly touching you— [*grabs* SUSAN*'s neck*]
SUSAN Lea' me alone!

[SUSAN *pushes* BINNIE *away.* BINNIE *falls on the ground, bumping her elbow*]

BINNIE Ow!

SUSAN Just leave me alone, Binnie, okay?
BINNIE You hurt me!
SUSAN I did not.
BINNIE You did so.
SUSAN Not very much.
BINNIE Kiss it better.

[BINNIE *shoves her elbow at* SUSAN, *who rolls her eyes, crosses away*]

SUSAN Binnie, Eleanor's right, you know, you're so—little.
BINNIE [*follows her, elbow foremost*] Come on! Pleeeze?
SUSAN It's childish, you know.

[BINNIE *stands waiting.* SUSAN *kisses elbow*]

BINNIE Okay watch, I'm gonna paralyze you without hardly—
SUSAN *Nooo!!*

[*Pause*]

BINNIE I wanna play with somebody.
SUSAN I don't feel like playing right now, okay?
BINNIE I didn't go running off to watch the stupid gymnastics. I stayed with you. So play with me.
SUSAN You only stayed 'cause you weren't allowed to go.
BINNIE Well, same with you!
SUSAN I know!
BINNIE So let's play! I'll race you to the top of the jungle gym.

SUSAN Why couldn't I go with them? Why doesn't she want me to go with them? If I was on the team and she wanted to go, I'd take her along. I'd *make* the team take her along.

BINNIE She's mean.

SUSAN Don't say that. She's your sister.

BINNIE I know she's my sister. She's mean anyway. [*pause*] Hey, you know what to do to her?

SUSAN What?

BINNIE Don't give her any of your puppies!

SUSAN We weren't gonna anyway.

BINNIE Give me two of the puppies, and don't give her any!

SUSAN Binnie look I have to check with my father who we give them to, okay?

BINNIE Okay well tell him to let me have two. That way I'll be able to cuddle one in each arm and she won't have any and she'll *cry* and *cry* …

[BINNIE *imitates* ELEANOR, *sobbing at* SUSAN's *feet*]

SUSAN [*reluctantly amused*] Knock it off!

BINNIE That way you can get back at her!

SUSAN Terrific!

[*Pause. Things are cheering up slightly*]

BINNIE How old are they now?

SUSAN The puppies? Well, how old were they yesterday?

BINNIE Eight days.

SUSAN So how old are they today?

BINNIE Nine days, you don't have to treat me like I'm a dummy, you know.

SUSAN I know, sorry.
BINNIE Just 'cause Eleanor does!
SUSAN [*laughing with her*] I know!
BINNIE Are they still as cute? The puppies?
SUSAN Yeah.
BINNIE How's the tiny little white one?
SUSAN 'Kay.
BINNIE I think you should call her Snowy. They got their eyes open yet?
SUSAN No, not till tomorrow prob'ly.
BINNIE I bet they're so cute.
SUSAN Yeah, but they don't even look like dogs yet. 'Cause their eyes are all closed. They look like fat little rats or something.
BINNIE Like this? [*does imitation*]
SUSAN [*amused*] Kind of. All they do is suck milk out of Muffin. Muffin's the mommy dog.
BINNIE *I* know Muffin.
SUSAN Oh yeah.
BINNIE So, uh, how long do they have to wait till their eyes are open?
SUSAN Ten days. They're deaf too, when they're born, you know.
BINNIE Deaf too? Blind and deaf? The poor things.
SUSAN Yeah—but it must be neat to be a little puppy dog and to open your eyes for the very first time. Can you imagine? If you didn't know you were blind— [*puts her hands over BINNIE's eyes*] and deaf— [*covers BINNIE's ears*] and all of a sudden you started to see— [*uncovers eyes*] and hear— [*uncovers ears*] It'd be so excellent, eh?
BINNIE [*gazing about on a new world*] Yeahh. Ooh.

[*Silence*]

SUSAN You know what? I wasn't gonna tell you.
BINNIE What?
SUSAN Well, the tiny little white one?
BINNIE Snowy? That's the one *I* want.
SUSAN Well—like, every litter of puppies, there's one called the runt. 'Cause it's the littlest and weakest. Well, in these puppies, Snowy's the runt. She can't hardly get at Muffin's milk. The others just push her out of the way 'cause she's so little.
BINNIE That's mean.
SUSAN Yeah, but they don't even know they're doing it. They just want theirs, that's all. [*pause*] The thing is—like—she might die.

[*Pause*]

BINNIE Die?
SUSAN Yeah. The others are all healthy, though. They'll be fine.
BINNIE Yeah—but Snowy was the—
SUSAN [*gently*] Binnie, you haven't even seen her.
BINNIE I know.
SUSAN Daddy says that's the way it works sometimes. The big ones are the ones that get everything.
BINNIE Yeah—all the big brothers and sisters.
SUSAN He says it's the law of the jungle.
BINNIE The law of the jungle? That's the law around *here*. That's the law of the jungle gym.
SUSAN You wanna skip? Let's skip, okay?
BINNIE Okay. What do you wanna do?

[*They get ready to skip*]

SUSAN Let's do 'Spanish Dancers,' we haven't done that one in a long time.

[*They skip*]

SUSAN & BINNIE Spanish Dancers, do the splits, splits, splits.
Spanish Dancers, do the kicks, kicks, kicks.
Spanish Dancers, turn a-round, round, round.
Spanish Dancers, touch the ground, ground, ground.
Spanish Dancers, get outa this town!
T! O! Double-U! N!

[*They end the skip, giggling. Pause*]

BINNIE It's not true what Eleanor said. That's a good rope.
SUSAN I know.
BINNIE You coming back here after school tomorrow?
SUSAN I dunno.
BINNIE Eleanor said she'd give you a gymnastics lesson.
SUSAN I know.
BINNIE I wish she'd give *me* a gymnastics lesson.
SUSAN Well, let's both come and maybe she will.
BINNIE Really?
SUSAN Sure.
BINNIE Okay! 'Kay, bye!
SUSAN Bye, Binnie! See you tomorrow!

[*They run off in different directions. Pause. Lighting change to indicate a new day, if there's lighting.*]

Enter ELEANOR *wearing a different outfit from the day before—tights, leotard, short pleated skirt—and walking as if on a balance beam. Takes a pose of readiness for a gymnastics routine*]

ELEANOR And then—the crowd gets all quiet—because here comes the most famous and beautiful gymnast in the world: Eleanor Garvey—me!—and she comes out looking so gorgeous that everybody is having an absolute fit. And once again she goes into her world-famous routine.

[ELEANOR *starts slowly, with limbers and walkovers. Maintains running commentary*]

Oh, she's perfect! She's never done it so well! The judges are falling on the floor, practically! The judges are, um, Wesley Crusher from 'Star Trek'—and Tom Cruise—and the guy who plays Doogie Howser. [*may be updated to keep pace with rapidly changing female preteen iconography*] And they're just—they're all falling madly in love with her!

[*She speeds up her routines with handsprings and cartwheels, if possible—perhaps some parallel-bar work*]

All her friends in the bleachers are just knocked out—Mavis O'Connell and Andrea Marcus are so jealous they can't stand it—and—Mike Grzeda from Grade Six—Mike Grzeda's sitting in the first row—crying—'cause he loves me so much!

[*Enter* SUSAN *and* BINNIE *separately, also dressed differently from before,* SUSAN *with skipping rope. They are behind* ELEANOR, *who is unaware of them. They close in, whisper and giggle, as* ELEANOR *continues*]

And now—the judges' decisions. [*completes routine, stands in position*] Wesley Crusher gives her—a ten out of ten! Yaaay! Tom Cruise gives her a ten and blows her a kiss! Yaaay! And the guy who plays Doogie Howser gives her—amazing! He's actually—he's going to give her—
BINNIE   *Two point five!*

[BINNIE *and* SUSAN *break up.* ELEANOR *turns, furious*]

Two and a half! Two and a half out of ten!
ELEANOR   Shut up! You shut your little mouth!

[ELEANOR *chases* BINNIE *around the jungle gym*]

SUSAN   Okay, okay!
ELEANOR   I'll kill you, I swear I'll kill you!
SUSAN   [*blocking* ELEANOR] Calm down!

[ELEANOR *comes to a stop.* BINNIE *cowers a safe distance behind* SUSAN]

ELEANOR   [*low, vicious*] Boy, are you ever in trouble. Mom said *four-thirty* you had to be home yesterday. So when didja get home? A *quarter past five!* Was she ever mad!
BINNIE   [*subdued*] So what.
ELEANOR   So she practically called the police!
BINNIE   Well, you didn't get home until nine-thirty!

ELEANOR Well, I was allowed! You weren't! She was so mad at Binnie this morning you know what she did?

SUSAN What?

ELEANOR She made *me* have to take *care* of her all afternoon. I have to *play* with her. I bet Olympic gymnasts never play with their baby sisters. [*performs on parallel bars*]

BINNIE You looked dumb, talking to yourself like that.

ELEANOR I didn't! I was psyching myself up! It was a pep talk! It's an important part of practising. Anybody can just talk to themselves.

SUSAN [*admiring a difficult move of* ELEANOR*'s*] But anybody can't do that, eh? You're getting good at it, you know, Eleanor, you're getting really good.

ELEANOR [*anger gone*] Oh, you think this is something, you should have seen the stuff they were doing yesterday.

SUSAN Yesterday?

ELEANOR At the Provincials!

SUSAN Oh yeah.

ELEANOR [*chattering away in all innocence*] They were so excellent, Susan!

SUSAN That's nice.

ELEANOR And afterwards, we all went out to a restaurant—our whole team and Miss Larson.

SUSAN And Jo-Anne.

ELEANOR And Paul and David. Oh, they were so funny! You shoulda been there.

SUSAN Yeah, I shoulda been there, Eleanor.

ELEANOR [*clues in*] Oh. Uh—I'm sorry you didn't come. I think it would have been okay. With everybody.

SUSAN I told you that yesterday!

[*Pause*]

ELEANOR So, like, are you here for a lesson now?
SUSAN No. [*skips*]
BINNIE You're not?
SUSAN *No.*
ELEANOR I could give you a lesson if you want.
BINNIE Yeah!
SUSAN Forget it.
ELEANOR I could teach you some floor tumbling. How about a handspring? You wanna learn a handspring?
BINNIE I do.
SUSAN [*beginning a favourite routine*] Who do?
BINNIE [*picking it up instantly*] You do.
SUSAN I do what? —No, no, wait a sec.
ELEANOR Oh, don't start that, it goes on forever.
SUSAN Start over, start over. You remind me of a lady.
BINNIE What lady?
SUSAN The lady with the power.
BINNIE What power?
SUSAN The power of voodoo.
BINNIE Who do?
SUSAN You do.
BINNIE I do what?
SUSAN [*both accelerating*] You remind me of a lady!
BINNIE What lady!
SUSAN Lady with the power!
BINNIE What power!
SUSAN Power of voodoo!
BINNIE Who do!
SUSAN You do!

[*Somewhere hereabouts, or soon after, the routine speeds up and burns out into giggling chaos*]

ELEANOR Would you stop being so childish? [*pause*] If that's the way you're gonna be, never mind. I won't give you a lesson.

SUSAN Okay then, don't gimme a lesson. See if I care.

[*Silence. Climbing and skipping activities.* BINNIE *runs to* ELEANOR, *tugs at her, is rebuffed. Runs to* SUSAN, *pokes at her, is rebuffed*]

BINNIE This is sure stupid.

SUSAN What is?

BINNIE Eleanor wants to give you a lesson an' you want Eleanor to give you a lesson an' so do I an' nobody's doing it.

ELEANOR You'll never get to join the team if you don't take lessons.

SUSAN What makes you think I want to join your team anyway?

ELEANOR You want to.

SUSAN Oh, yeah, Eleanor, tell me about it. How come you want to give me lessons anyway? What do you care?

ELEANOR I wouldn't mind it if you were on the team.

SUSAN You wouldn't *mind? Thanks.*

ELEANOR I'd like it, okay? I'd like you to be on the team, all right?

SUSAN [*pleased*] Finally.

ELEANOR When you're a little older, though.

SUSAN [*displeased*] When I'm a little older, though! You're ten and I'm nine! It's not that big a difference!

ELEANOR I didn't say it was. But you're not ready yet. You need lessons. That's why I want to.
SUSAN I think you like giving lessons so you can show off. I think you like having somebody around that you can pretend you're the big-shot teacher to.
BINNIE Who cares why, let's just do it!
ELEANOR Look, do you want a dumb lesson or not!
BINNIE *I* do!
SUSAN Yeah, yeah, I want a stupid lesson!
ELEANOR Well, all right then!
SUSAN [*amused*] All right!
BINNIE [*enthused*] All right!

[BINNIE *giggles and jumps around with excitement.* ELEANOR *casually pushes her out of the way as she and* SUSAN *get into place*]

But I'm taking the lesson too.
ELEANOR You are not.
SUSAN Oh, come on, Eleanor, let her.

[*Pause*]

ELEANOR All right. Today, we're gonna learn a handspring.
BINNIE A handspring, a handspring!

[BINNIE *chortles and leaps around.* ELEANOR *tries to freeze her with a glare.* BINNIE *stifles her excitement and stands embarrassed, twitching slightly*]

ELEANOR [*to* SUSAN] You'll have to do a warm-up for this, but first I'll show you what it looks like. You have

to do a regular handstand, but you kick your feet up extra hard, and I'll catch your ankles. I'll do it first. You spot me, Susan, okay?
BINNIE Stick spots all over her.
ELEANOR Be ready to grab my ankles.
SUSAN 'Kay.
ELEANOR Watch.

[ELEANOR *does a handstand, kicks up hard.* SUSAN *grabs her ankles*]

SUSAN Great!
BINNIE Your skirt, your skirt!

[*As* ELEANOR *is upside down, her skirt falls 'up'—certainly not for the first time, and with no improper effect. But* BINNIE *rushes in and tries to hold the skirt up over the revealed area*]

ELEANOR [*collapsing out of the handstand*] Aaahh! Binnie, what are you doing!
BINNIE I'm helping, I'm helping!
ELEANOR Great. Okay. Now for your warm-up, Susan. [*takes spotter's position*] It's just a handstand like you've done lots of times. Only kick as hard as you can. And don't worry about falling, I'll catch your feet.
BINNIE She's lying, she's gonna let you fall on your spine and die!
ELEANOR [*ignoring her*] You ready?
SUSAN Uh, yeah—
ELEANOR Okay go!

[SUSAN *does a handstand and kicks up hard and correctly.* ELEANOR *catches her ankles*]

Perfect. Really good.

[BINNIE *charges in, uncovers* SUSAN*'s tummy, and blows into her bare stomach with loud, flatulent effect.* SUSAN *screams and falls out of her handstand*]

SUSAN Aaahh, *gross!*

[SUSAN *wipes her hand on her stomach and chases* BINNIE, *trying to wipe the mostly imaginary spit off on* BINNIE*'s arm. Much amusement.* ELEANOR *intervenes*]

ELEANOR Binnie, lay off! Stop *bugging* everybody! If you don't want to take a lesson, don't get in the way of those who are!
BINNIE I wanna take a lesson!
ELEANOR Well, okay, you watch for now. [*seats her*] Please, Bin, be nice, okay?
BINNIE [*puzzled*] Okay.
ELEANOR Okay, now we do the full handspring. You do the full handspring the exact same way.
BINNIE [*stepping in*] Don't I get to do a warm-up?
ELEANOR Oh. Sure. You can do a forward roll.

[ELEANOR *efficiently pushes* BINNIE *into a forward roll and out of their way*]

Now in the handspring, you arch your back and you go right over. It looks like this. [*performs handspring*]

SUSAN *Wooo!* [*intimidated*] Ooh, I dunno.
ELEANOR You can learn to do that.
SUSAN No I can't.
ELEANOR Yes you can!
SUSAN Nooo ...
ELEANOR I can tell, Susan, I've watched you. I'll teach you. You'll be really good, I know you will.
SUSAN Yeah?
BINNIE Me too!
ELEANOR Okay, take up your position.

[SUSAN *takes up standing position,* ELEANOR *spotter's position*]

Now go into your handstand and I'll just ease you over.
SUSAN Ee I'm nervous.
ELEANOR I know you can do it. And I've spotted lots and lots of times.
BINNIE Yeah and they always fell on their head.
ELEANOR Binnie!
BINNIE Then they die.
ELEANOR Could you let the gymnast concentrate, please!

[SUSAN *is getting the giggles*]

BINNIE There's a whole corner of the graveyard, it says, 'These People Were Spotted by Eleanor, Boo Hoo Hoo,' hee hee hee—

[SUSAN *cracks up*]

ELEANOR Come on, Susan. She's just being obnoxious.

Keep your arms straight and stretch out your whole body and you'll be great.
BINNIE A little bit dead, maybe, but great.
ELEANOR Binnie, you are making this impossible!
BINNIE Sorreee. Hee hee hee.
SUSAN [*groans through her giggles*] Binnie, stop it!
BINNIE Go for it, Susan! [*tickles* SUSAN, *who screams*] Okay, outa my way, Useless, I'll show you how.
ELEANOR She isn't being funny, it's just silly!
SUSAN I know—
BINNIE Spot me, Eleanor, here I come!

[ELEANOR *turns her back on* BINNIE. BINNIE *jumps on* ELEANOR*'s back and rides her, hollering*]

ELEANOR Binnie! Get off!
BINNIE Yahooo!

[ELEANOR *throws* BINNIE *to the ground and grabs her in a clinch.* ELEANOR *screams in uncontrolled anger.* BINNIE *is silent.* SUSAN *watches, shocked*]

ELEANOR You! You mess up everything! You make fun of everything! You ruin everything!

[ELEANOR *finds some control, lets go of* BINNIE, *crosses away from her.* BINNIE *is frightened, hugging herself, near tears. Pause*]

Just don't you start blubbering. Just don't.
BINNIE I'm not gonna start blubbering.
ELEANOR [*to* SUSAN] What are you gawking at?

SUSAN I'm allowed.
ELEANOR You don't know what it's like to have a sister. Like her. You're lucky. She drives me crazy.
BINNIE You're already crazy.
ELEANOR Aw, Binnie—
SUSAN You get along sometimes. You're super nice to each other sometimes.
ELEANOR Not very often.
BINNIE [*to* SUSAN] Last week she hit me right in the face. Pow.
SUSAN I know, I was there.
BINNIE Oh yeah.
ELEANOR [*embarrassed*] Let's not go over that again, okay? Bin, are you okay?
BINNIE Who, me? I'm perfect.
ELEANOR Hug?

[*They cross to each other and embrace carefully*]

BINNIE Don't squeeze too hard, my arms'll fall off.
ELEANOR Great comfort you are.

[*They disengage from the hug. Pause*]

BINNIE Both of you stop looking at me. Let's do the lesson some more.
SUSAN Yeah!
BINNIE Yeah it's my turn now, you gotta teach me a handspring. But Susan's gotta spot me though, because if you spot me I'll probably fall down and get killed. Heh heh.

[*Not much response to the joke this time, except for a wan smile from* SUSAN. *Pause*]

ELEANOR Binnie I'm sorry, but I think maybe you better go play somewhere else for a while.
BINNIE Oh Eleanor, come on.
ELEANOR All you want to do is fool around and get in the way. I can't teach. I lose my temper and this is what happens.
SUSAN She was just having a little fun.
ELEANOR Well, it isn't fun. It's silliness. Working on gymnastics is fun, doing it right is fun.
BINNIE Working is fun?
ELEANOR Yes, if you love it. I'm sorry. But if Binnie stays, we can't have a lesson.
SUSAN Aw, please? I wanna learn it, I really do. I'm sorry I laughed. Let's try it again.
ELEANOR Okay, but I think Binnie has to leave first.
BINNIE Susan wants me to stay! Don't you, Susan?

[*Pause*]

SUSAN Well, I do want to learn the handspring—
ELEANOR Fine. When Binnie leaves.
BINNIE Eleanor, you're snobby.
ELEANOR I'm not! You think if I'm not paying attention to you, I'm being snobby. But I can't teach with you making fun like that. Nobody could, not even Miss Larson.
BINNIE Yeah, well, that's too bad. 'Cause you have to play with me or I'll tell Mommy. You got to take care of me.
ELEANOR [*fists clenched*] I'll take care of you, all right.

SUSAN Binnie, you don't have to go far away. Just over there somewhere, other end of the playground.

BINNIE Whyyy!

SUSAN Well, she's right, you know, it isn't much fun with you horsing around.

BINNIE You thought it was fun. You were laughing your head off!

SUSAN Yeah, but I wasn't doing the handspring, was I?

BINNIE I can stay here if I want to. It's a free country.

SUSAN Oh, Binnie, you're always hanging around being goofy. You always make fun of everything and it just gets all silly and we never get anything done. Eleanor and I never get to be alone, you know. Can't you just leave us alone for once?

BINNIE Please let me stay. I'll be your best friend, Susan.

SUSAN Well, that's sort of what I'm afraid of.

[ELEANOR *hides her amusement, but* BINNIE *sees it*]

BINNIE You two are so crazy about each other. You're so in love with yourselves it makes me wanna puke. Why don't you two get *married?*

SUSAN Very funny.

BINNIE Well, you're acting just like Eleanor when she went to the gym contest! You couldn't go, so I stayed and cheered you up! And now you're saying the same thing she said! Thanks a lot, Susan! [*starting to cry*] I hate it here! Everybody picks on everybody—but *everybody* picks on *me* 'cause I'm the *littlest!* [*full wail*] I hate you guys! I hate it here! I hate it!

[BINNIE *runs off, in tears. Silence*]

ELEANOR Well, anyway. Handspring?

[SUSAN *is still looking after* BINNIE]

Susan?
SUSAN Okay.
ELEANOR Take up your position. Don't worry about her, she's doing it on purpose.

[SUSAN *takes up position, and* ELEANOR *spotting position, as before*]

Okay don't be scared, just push yourself into a really fast handstand. And arch your back.
SUSAN This is scary.
ELEANOR Yeah, but if you fight it you'll curl up and land on your bum. So arch your back. I'll carry you over.
SUSAN [*deep breath*] Okay.

[SUSAN *goes into the handstand.* ELEANOR *helps her over.* SUSAN *commits the commonest error and doesn't arch enough: she goes over stiffly, is leaning backwards when her feet hit the floor, and falls on her rear*]

Aaahh! Oy.
ELEANOR You okay?
SUSAN Yeah. Yeah. But that was terrible.
ELEANOR Yeah, it sure was. You didn't arch enough. You gotta get up and try it again right away.
SUSAN [*gets up, looks off for* BINNIE] Where'd she go?
ELEANOR Who cares, let her cry. She's just being a baby.
SUSAN [*stares at* ELEANOR] No. You know what she's

being? She's being the runt. It's true. She's like the runt of the litter, and we're like the other puppies, and we just keep shoving her out of—
ELEANOR Susan, will you pay attention!
SUSAN I was!
ELEANOR Okay, let's see you do it, then!
SUSAN Okay, then!

[SUSAN *does her handspring with* ELEANOR *spotting. This one is better, but again ends with her leaning back.* ELEANOR *holds her up for a moment*]

ELEANOR See? See? You're doing it all wrong! You're still too straight with your back!
SUSAN [*annoyed*] Lemme up. [*gets up, looks off for* BINNIE]
ELEANOR You're not arching enough. You're not paying attention at all! You're too busy worrying about that little runt Binnie.
SUSAN I'm worrying about the law of the jungle gym.
ELEANOR The what?
SUSAN Something Binnie said.
ELEANOR Well, never mind, whatever you're worrying about, it isn't your handspring.
SUSAN Okay, okay, I'll work on the *handspring*.
ELEANOR So go ahead!
SUSAN All right!

[*Fuelled by anger, she executes the handspring, very nicely. Comes out of it surprised*]

I did it. [*brief pause*] It was perfect.
ELEANOR Well, okay, not bad.

SUSAN [*becoming elated as it sinks in*] It wasn't not bad, it was perfect! [*calls off*] Hey! Binnie!

ELEANOR [*pulls on her arm*] Leave her alone!

SUSAN Bin-nee! Wanna see a perfect handspring?

ELEANOR Leave her alone! Do it again!

SUSAN Do you mind if we show your sister at least?

ELEANOR We are not playing with her now, we are doing a lesson.

SUSAN That was just till I learned it. Now I want to show her I learned it.

ELEANOR You haven't learned it! You only did it once! Get back in position! [*shoves* SUSAN]

SUSAN Stop being so bossy!

ELEANOR Well I have to, Susan, or else you won't do it. What are you doing?

SUSAN I'm trying to wonder where she went, can't I even do that? Your Majesty?

ELEANOR Not when you're doing gymnastics!

SUSAN You think the whole world is gymnastics.

ELEANOR You have to, if you're ever gonna be a great athlete.

SUSAN Yeah, well, there's more important things than stupid gymnastics!

ELEANOR Name one!

SUSAN The runt. The puppy that might die. One little puppy is more important than all the gymnastics in the world.

ELEANOR Who the heck is talking about puppies? That is the stupidest thing!

SUSAN Yeah, well, a great athlete would care about stuff like that!

ELEANOR [*shoves* SUSAN] Would you get back in position?

SUSAN She'd care, if her sister was always being shoved out of the way like we do!

ELEANOR I care about my sister, but right now we're doing this! [*shoves her into position*]

SUSAN You play with me and Binnie 'cause we're smaller, that's all! [*shoves* ELEANOR *hard*] And younger!

ELEANOR [*grabs* SUSAN's *head*] Neck straight! Shoulders down!

SUSAN So you can push us around! And feel more important! 'Cause you're such a snob! [*shoves again*]

ELEANOR It's because the two of you are such babies! You'll never learn to do it right! You're too immature!

SUSAN [*yelling*] You only play with me and Binnie 'cause Mavis O'Connell and Andrea Marcus won't play with you, 'cause they're good at gymnastics and they told me *you're rotten! Rotten rotten rotten!*

[*They join battle, in a clinch, grappling in grim silence. They topple to the floor and roll around briefly. Then* ELEANOR *twists* SUSAN's *arm.* SUSAN *screams, clutches her arm in an unnatural position.* ELEANOR *jumps away from her, watches in horror*]

ELEANOR It was an accident!

[SUSAN *wails*]

Besides, it was your fault!

[SUSAN *wails*]

I'm sorry! What do you want from me!

BINNIE [*runs on*] What happened? Hey Susan, what did she do to you? Hey Eleanor, whatcha do to her?
ELEANOR I'm *sorry!*
BINNIE Boy, Susan, are you ever loud. I could hear you way the other end of the playground.
SUSAN Lea' me alooone.
BINNIE What'd she do to your arm?
SUSAN Sprained my shoulder!
ELEANOR I'm sorry! I didn't mean it!
BINNIE Really? She sprained it?
SUSAN [*miserable*] Prob'ly.
BINNIE Can you move it? Try and move it.
ELEANOR You're not supposed to move it!
BINNIE You're supposed to try, and if you can't move it then you have to go to the hospital, okay?
ELEANOR The hospital?
SUSAN Yeah.
BINNIE Try and move it.
SUSAN Here goes. [*tries*] Ooww.
BINNIE It's sprained.
ELEANOR No! No it isn't!
SUSAN Yes it is!
BINNIE Yeah you have to go to the hospital!

[BINNIE *carefully lifts the neck of* SUSAN's *shirt to observe the wound*]

ELEANOR I'm sorry. I'm sorry.
SUSAN Y'are not!
ELEANOR I am so. I didn't do it on purpose, you know.
SUSAN You did so!
ELEANOR I did not!

SUSAN Liar liar!
BINNIE I think it's getting swollen.
ELEANOR Really?
SUSAN I'm going to the hospital.
ELEANOR Lemme come with you. I'll walk you home.
SUSAN You'd only crowd up the ambulance. [*exit*]

[*Silence*]

ELEANOR Binnie? She's not gonna need a cast or anything. Is she? I mean I only bent it a tiny bit.
BINNIE I dunno. Don't worry about it.

[*Pause*]

ELEANOR I thought you were gonna make some dumb joke. Say she was gonna die or something.
BINNIE I don't always make dumb jokes, you know.
ELEANOR Most of the time.
BINNIE It's funny, eh. When you don't want to be with somebody it doesn't matter. But when they don't want to be with you, then it matters, eh?
ELEANOR What do you know about it, you're too young.
BINNIE Yeah, well, you're too old, that's your problem.
  [*climbs jungle gym*]
ELEANOR You don't know what you're talking about.
BINNIE Oh, stuff a sock in it, Eleanor.
ELEANOR Everybody hates me!
BINNIE [*hanging upside down, sings*] Nobody loves me, everybody hates me,
  I'm gonna eat some wo-o-o-orms—
ELEANOR Quiet.

JOHN LAZARUS

Anne Clark (ELEANOR) and Barbara Duncan (BINNIE)

BINNIE Big fat juicy ones, long slim slimy ones,
Itsy-bitsy fuzzy-wuzzy wo-o-o-orms.
ELEANOR Don't!
BINNIE First you bite their heads off,
Then you suck their guts out,
Oh how they wiggle and they squi-i-i-irm—
ELEANOR Bin-neee! Will you please shut up!

[*Silence*]

BINNIE I do so know what I'm talking about.
ELEANOR About what?
BINNIE I know all about not being friends any more. Everybody's always stopped being my friend.
ELEANOR If you keep singing that thing, I'm not surprised.
BINNIE I never decide to be somebody's friend or not. The other person decides.
ELEANOR Yeah, but you go along with it.
BINNIE I'm ascared not to. I'm ascared if I don't go along with it I won't have any friends at all.
ELEANOR Oh, you never know, Bin. You could have a friend.
BINNIE Yeah?
ELEANOR Somebody weird enough might come along.
BINNIE I've decided about you, though.
ELEANOR [*reluctantly*] What do you mean?
BINNIE Well, I wouldn't want to be friends with you, that's all.
ELEANOR Well, too bad. We're stuck with each other. For life.
BINNIE I know. But if I had a choice, I wouldn't be your friend.

ELEANOR [*reluctantly*] Why not?
BINNIE I don't like how you treat people sometimes. I mean sometimes you're really nice. But sometimes you send people to play someplace else and you sprain their shoulders and stuff and it gets kind of boring.
ELEANOR So? I wouldn't want to be your friend either.
BINNIE I know. But I wouldn't be your friend even if you wanted to. You could beg me and beg me and I still wouldn't be your friend. In fact I'm thinking of not being your sister any more. I wouldn't mind being Wesley Crusher's sister, that'd be fun.

[*With flatulent motor sound-effects,* BINNIE *takes the controls of the* Enterprise]

ELEANOR I could make you be my friend if I wanted to.
BINNIE Could not.
ELEANOR I could too.
BINNIE You can't make somebody be your friend. You can only just scare them, that's all.
ELEANOR I could if I wanted to!
BINNIE Yeah, eh? By spraining their shoulder, that's how? That's great, Eleanor.

[*Silence. Enter* SUSAN, *slowly, holding her arm. Crosses past* ELEANOR *to* BINNIE]

SUSAN [*quietly*] Hi, Binnie.
BINNIE Hi.
SUSAN My father says it isn't sprained. I don't have to go.
ELEANOR Oh, thank goodness. Thank goodness.

SUSAN It's just *badly twisted*, that's all. [*to* ELEANOR] Anyway, I came back for my skipping rope. Can I have it back now, or are you gonna strangle Binnie with it?

[ELEANOR *hands skipping rope to* SUSAN, *turns aside and begins to cry*]

[*to* BINNIE] What's with her?
BINNIE I dunno.
ELEANOR [*crying*] How come I'm always the bad guy? You guys, I don't know what you want from me! First you say I boss you around, but when I try to be nice to you and I teach you gymnastics, well, everybody laughs at me and you say I get pushy. Well, you know, if you just push back now and then maybe I wouldn't push so hard. At least it'd be over.
SUSAN It's over.
ELEANOR No! All I did was twist your arm a little and now you won't be my friend for as long as I live! You call that 'over'? If you could just hurt me back, then we could be even and we could still be friends.
SUSAN But I don't want to hurt you back.
ELEANOR What if somebody wanted you to?
SUSAN Why would anybody want you to hurt them?
ELEANOR So we'd be more even.
BINNIE You know what, I think she wants you to hurt her.
SUSAN Eleanor? Do you want me to hurt you?

[ELEANOR *shrugs*]

BINNIE Yeah, you know, I think she wants you to hurt her!
SUSAN Uh, do you want me to twist your arm, or what?

[ELEANOR, *her back to* SUSAN, *lifts an arm*]

Uh, well, Eleanor, I think maybe I'm gonna sort of twist your arm a little now, if you don't mind.
ELEANOR Get it over with.

[ELEANOR *shuts her eyes, grits her teeth.* SUSAN *takes* ELEANOR's *wrist between thumb and one finger and turns it slightly*]

Go ahead, get it *over* with.
SUSAN That was it.
ELEANOR That was it? That was how you hurt a person? That was pathetic!
SUSAN I'm sorry.
ELEANOR If you're really gonna get back at me you got to twist harder. [*steels herself again*]
SUSAN I don't believe this. Okay. Kung fooo! [*imitating* BINNIE's *kung fu*] Hyah! Hah! Chung! Ka-Pow! Kee-yah! [*culminates in a tiny judo chop on* ELEANOR's *arm*] There. 'Kay?
ELEANOR That is nothing! You got to twist! That didn't even hurt!
SUSAN But I don't want to hurt you.
ELEANOR I hurt you, didn't I?
SUSAN You sure did.
ELEANOR Then you have to hurt me as much as I hurt you.
SUSAN I have to?
ELEANOR If we're gonna be even. If we're gonna be friends.
SUSAN Nearly sprain your shoulder and everything?
ELEANOR Just will you get it over with!

Barbara Duncan (BINNIE), Wendy Noel (SUSAN), Anne Clark (ELEANOR)

SUSAN Okay then, you asked for it.

[SUSAN *twists* ELEANOR*'s arm in earnest.* ELEANOR *yells*]

Enough?
ELEANOR No.
SUSAN Okay. [*twists harder*] Give up yet?
ELEANOR Nnn—no!
SUSAN Okay— [*prepares to twist harder still*]
BINNIE [*running in between them*] Come on, you guys, cut it out! Stop hurting my sister.
SUSAN She wants me to.
BINNIE But I don't want you to.
SUSAN Well, I didn't want to in the first place.
ELEANOR Well, how else are we going to get even?
SUSAN It's okay, you know. It's okay. My arm doesn't

even hurt any more, really. I hereby officially forgive you, Eleanor.

[SUSAN *bows formally. General easing of tension*]

ELEANOR Were you really gonna twist my arm hard?
SUSAN Yeah, Eleanor. I was gonna snap it right off, take it home and eat it for supper.

[ELEANOR *and* BINNIE *express disgust*]

ELEANOR Well, what are we gonna do now?
SUSAN [*suddenly remembers*] Guess what!
BINNIE & ELEANOR What! What!
SUSAN Uh, guess!
BINNIE Give us a hint.
SUSAN It has to do with something small.
BINNIE Eyeglasses!
SUSAN No.
ELEANOR You're getting a wristwatch.
SUSAN No!
BINNIE Toes!
ELEANOR This is dumb. Give us another hint.
SUSAN This is a giveaway.

[SUSAN *imitates* BINNIE*'s imitation of a nine-day-old puppy*]

BINNIE The puppies.
SUSAN Yeah! Two of them have got their eyes open and Dad says you can come see them today!
ELEANOR Really? Well, let's go!

BINNIE The puppies the puppies the puppies!

[*They begin to exit with much ad lib noise and excitement*]

SUSAN Hey you guys, you can't yell around the puppies, okay?
ELEANOR [*yelling*] Who's yelling!

[*Exeunt*]

NOT SO DUMB

Production History

Not So Dumb was first produced by Green Thumb Theatre for Young People, at the École Jules Quesnel, Vancouver, on September 20, 1984, with the following cast:

BINNIE, Wendy Donaldson
ROCKY, Thomas Hunt
VICTOR, Stephen Aberle

Director: Dennis Foon
Set and Costume Designer: Marti Wright
Stage Manager: Michael Cunningham

Subsequently it received three more productions by Green Thumb, two by Wellington Teachers' College (New Zealand) and Starving Artists' Theatre (Hawaii), and single productions by Neptune Theatre (Halifax), Young People's Theatre (Toronto), Magnus Theatre Lab (Thunder Bay), Actors Showcase (Winnipeg), Columbus Junior Theatre (Ohio), Grand Theatre (London, Ontario), and Missoula Children's Theatre (Montana). *Not So Dumb* has received a Jessie Award and a Chalmers Award.

Acknowledgements

My thanks to Dennis Foon, Green Thumb Theatre, and Robert Metcalfe, for workshopping and helping to develop this script; to Young People's Theatre of Toronto, for taking time out of their playwrights' workshop in spring of 1984 to work on the play; to Roman Piontkovsky, and the parents and children of the Vancouver Association for Children and Adults with Learning Disabilities; to Dr. Annaleise Robens; and to Mrs. Loveseth and Mr. Dean of False Creek Elementary School. Finally, my thanks to the original cast, for their many inspired improvisations, which helped to shape the script and became a part of it.

Characters

ROCKY a sloppily dressed boy, age ten.

BINNIE a bright, energetic girl, a joker, athletic, age ten. This is the **BINNIE** of *Schoolyard Games,* a couple of years later.

VICTOR seen by others, perhaps unfairly, as the class wimp, age ten.

Setting

A Learning Assistance Classroom in an elementary school. The walls are full of shelves of brightly coloured books and cartons of 'resource materials.' (Most of this is not functional, and can be glued in; it doesn't have to be naturalistic, either.) There is a door with a translucent window. Essential furniture includes a brightly striped filing cabinet, prominently marked 'CONFIDENTIAL,' and a teacher's desk. There is a blackboard, with a schedule of classes on it, including a listing that says, among other dates and names, 'WEDNESDAYS AND FRIDAYS (or any combination of weekdays including the weekday of the performance), BINNIE GARVEY AND RUPERT KEEFER.' There may also be a work table and chairs, and/or some large wooden blocks of furniture size. On one of the shelves near the door, there are several hand puppets. Pre-set among them are a Professor puppet, a Lion puppet, and a strange, furry, cross-eyed puppet known as the Sponge Beast.

BINNIE [*off*] Mrs. Smith! Mrs. Smi-i-ith! I finished my composition!

[*She enters, carrying her books and chattering happily*]

My parents said it was great an' even my sister likes it, an'—

[*Beat. It's clear Mrs. Smith is not here.* BINNIE *looks around*]

Where is she? Mrs. Smith?

[BINNIE *goes to the door, opens it—it opens outwards— and slams* ROCKY *in the face*]

ROCKY Oowww! [*holds onto his face, seeming genuinely hurt*]
BINNIE Rocky! Are you okay?
ROCKY [*emerges from behind his hand, honking*] Ar! Ar! Ar! ...
BINNIE Rock-ee! Mrs. Smith isn't here.
ROCKY I can see that, thanks.

[*They survey the room*]

BINNIE Whole room looks different without Mrs. Smith here.
ROCKY So where is she, anyways?

BINNIE *I* dunno. That's weird that she's not here. An' I got my composition finished an' everything. You think maybe something's wrong?
ROCKY Well, are we s'posed to have a class here, or what?
BINNIE I dunno. Uh—today's—what's today?
ROCKY [*names the day of performance*]?
BINNIE Yeah, right. An' classes are [ ]days an' Fridays. Right?
ROCKY Right.
BINNIE So we're here the right day.
ROCKY Right.
BINNIE This doesn't make sense. We must be getting something wrong. Why isn't she here!
ROCKY I dunno.
BINNIE I hate that! I hate when people change things!
ROCKY I know. Don't get so nervous about it.
BINNIE Okay, check the schedule.
ROCKY Aw, what for?
BINNIE Just to make sure she hasn't changed it. Like, put us on a different day.
ROCKY They never change our day.
BINNIE Well, just to make sure! I mean *something* isn't making sense.
ROCKY Okay, then, *you* check it.
BINNIE No, it's your job! Beginning of every Learning Assistance class, Rocky checks the schedule.
ROCKY I can't read it.
BINNIE You can read it.
ROCKY If I could read I wouldn't be taking these classes, would I!
BINNIE Rocky ... Don' act any stupider than you have to, okay?

ROCKY I don't have to read the schedule! I hate the schedule! You read the schedule!
BINNIE Okay, Rocky.
ROCKY All right.

[*She crosses to the board and peers abnormally closely at it, trying to find their own listing*]

BINNIE Okay, got it, Rock. The schedule says: '[ ]days and Fridays: Arnold Schwarzenegger an' Roseanne.' [*or whoever is current*]
ROCKY It does not!
BINNIE Does so!
ROCKY Does not.
BINNIE Does so.
ROCKY It doesn't! It says '[ ]days an' Fridays: Rocky an' Binnie!'
BINNIE Ha ha, ha ha! Made ya read it!
ROCKY No you didn't! I didn't even read it! I just remembered it.
BINNIE I knew that! You didn't fool me! 'Cause it doesn't say 'Rocky an' Binnie,' it says 'Binnie Garvey and Rupert Keefer.'
ROCKY '*Rupert*'?
BINNIE Yeah.
ROCKY Aw, no! I wish she wouldn't do that. Nobody calls me 'Rupert' 'cept Mrs. Smith.
BINNIE Rupert was some prince somewhere. 'Cause Prince Rupert's the name of a city.
ROCKY Yeah, well, good for him. How come she can call you 'Binnie,' but she can't call me 'Rocky'?
BINNIE Binnie's my official name.

ROCKY Lucky you didn't start out with a stupid name like 'Rupert.'

BINNIE Yeah, Rocky, it would be very weird if I was named 'Rupert.'

ROCKY I'm gonna change it.

BINNIE What?

ROCKY On the board. I'm gonna change it. I'm gonna put my real name. 'Rocky.'

BINNIE Great! Go for it!

[ROCKY *crosses to the blackboard. Finds his name, glances at* BINNIE, *who nods confirmation. Rubs it out and begins to draw a clumsy letter* R]

BINNIE Not like that—

ROCKY Don't tell me!

BINNIE I wasn't!

ROCKY Don't tell me nothin'! I know how to write my own name, 'kay.

[*He continues tracing and muttering.* BINNIE, *annoyed by this and bored, picks up the Sponge Beast puppet and puts it on. She begins to breathe wetly, as the Sponge Beast. She sneaks up on* ROCKY *and suddenly attacks him with the puppet*]

BINNIE [*as Sponge Beast*] Maschter! ... I am your Schponge Beascht! ... Maschter! ...

ROCKY [*yelps, brushes it away*] Argh! Get that thing offa me!

BINNIE Yesch, Maschter ...

ROCKY Ya shouldn't *spring* that thing on a guy, ya know.

BINNIE It's only a puppet. The Intergalactic Sponge Beast. [*makes schlurping noises*]

ROCKY Well, it's the grossest puppet I ever seen. 'S got fleas.
BINNIE It does not! Where? Oh.

[*She pretends to find a flea in the puppet's fur. Feeds it to the Sponge Beast. The Sponge Beast swallows it down and belches*]

Not any more!

[*She cuddles the Sponge Beast. Meanwhile,* ROCKY *has laboriously finished his name*]

ROCKY Hey, I finished it. In case anybody cares or anything.

[*They admire the handiwork: a loosely scrawled 'Rocky' sprawling amid the neatly written teacher's notes on the board*]

BINNIE You think she'll be mad?
ROCKY Who cares? It's my name, not hers. Ya know, I'm not taking her name an' changing it into 'Mrs. Rocky' or nothin'.
BINNIE [*chortles*] 'Mrs. Rocky.'
ROCKY Anyway, she oughta be happy. This's the firs' thing I've written on the board in like months. So? Whaddaya think?
BINNIE [*moves in close behind him, as if to get a good look*] Wait a second— Lemme see— [*attacks him with the Sponge Beast*] Schlurp schlurp schlurp schlurp schlurp!
ROCKY Bin-neee!

[*But the Sponge Beast will not let up, so* ROCKY *makes a grab for the Lion puppet, and it suddenly turns on* BINNIE, *growling ferociously.* BINNIE *screams in delighted terror, and* ROCKY *chases her around the room. She and the Sponge Beast hide behind the blocks, and* ROCKY *and the Lion stalk them*]

BINNIE I hear ya sneakin' up …

[ROCKY's *Lion comes at* BINNIE *over the top of the blocks. She squeals and runs across the room. Cornered, she pets the Sponge Beast to comfort it. Parodying her,* ROCKY *pets his Lion*]

Aw, that's not scary.

[*In response the Lion roars ferociously;* BINNIE *screams some more. Soon the Lion has the Sponge Beast cornered. It grabs the Sponge Beast in its jaws and yanks it off* BINNIE's *hand. It slams the Sponge Beast into the filing cabinet a few times—as* BINNIE *supplies Dying-Sponge-Beast noises—then drops it, dead, on top of the cabinet. It sniffs at the corpse for a moment, and then, satisfied that the Beast is dead, turns its attention to* BINNIE. *The Lion stalks* BINNIE *for a moment, and then attacks. But* BINNIE *responds by embracing the Lion in a maternal hug*]

Ooohhh … I just love baby lion cubs …

[*She hugs and kisses it. Disgusted,* ROCKY *pulls it away*]

ROCKY 'Ooh, I jus' love baby lion cubs … An' little puppy dogs and little baby kittens …' You're such a

sucker for babies, Binnie, it's disgusting.
BINNIE [*cheerfully*] Yeah, I know. I'm gonna have a dozen kids when I grow up.
ROCKY Yeah, right, a dozen little baby Binnies boppin' around in their diapers ...
BINNIE That's it. Of course. That's it, Rocky!
ROCKY What?
BINNIE She's having her baby!
ROCKY Oh!
BINNIE Yeah! That's what it is! She's having her baby, Mrs. Smith's having her baby!
ROCKY Is it time yet?
BINNIE Are you kidding? She's so pregnant she could hardly get in the door last time! She's having her baby!
ROCKY Or else she got lost on the way to the classroom.
BINNIE No no no no, she's having her baby! Yay, Mrs. *Smith!*
ROCKY She coulda got lost.
BINNIE She's having her baby!
ROCKY She got lost!
BINNIE [*dancing*] She's having her baby, she's having her baby, yay Mrs. Smith, she's having her baby— [*etc.*]
ROCKY [*dumps the waste-basket over* BINNIE*'s head*] She got lost!
BINNIE [*from within waste-basket*] Will you stop it? How could she get lost from the office to the classroom? The office is like two doors down!
ROCKY Well, she's L-D too, you know.
BINNIE No she's not.
ROCKY Sure she is. She told me. She nearly flunked out of school herself, she was so learning disabled. She was like me.

BINNIE Really?
ROCKY Yeah!
BINNIE [*peeking out of waste-basket*] That bad, huh? [*pulls it back over her head, but* ROCKY *takes no offence*]
ROCKY Yeah! That's why she started to teach learning disabled. She told me.
BINNIE You're kidding.
ROCKY So I figure she got lost on the way to the classroom.
BINNIE [*emerging from waste-basket*] Rocky, she's been coming here every day for the last two hundred years. She's not gonna get lost now. I mean she may be L-D, but she's not stupid.
ROCKY Go check.
BINNIE What? Go check if she's stupid?
ROCKY Go check if she's in the hall. Go outside an' give 'er a shout.

[*Beat. Then* BINNIE *exits and yells into the hall*]

BINNIE Mrs. Smi-i-i-i-i— [*pause. Speaking to someone, off*] Oh. Hi, Mr. Powers.

[ROCKY *frantically hides behind the door*]

No, sir, I was just looking for Mrs. Smith. I finished a composition, and I want her to— Yessir. I mean, no sir. I know. I won't, sir, I'll be quiet, sir, sorry, Mr. Powers sir. [*comes back into the classroom, humorously stifling herself*] Boy, am I in trouble now.
ROCKY What'd he say?
BINNIE What do you think? He told me there's a rule against screaming your head off in the halls. Surprise surprise.

ROCKY No, I mean about Mzz Smith.
BINNIE [*puzzled*] He didn't! He just went back in the Principal's Office.
ROCKY Well, he doesn't seem worried about her.
BINNIE Guess not. [*beat*] So let's do something!
ROCKY Like what?
BINNIE I dunno. I've never been here without a teacher before.
ROCKY Me neither.

[*Pause, as they try to think up some mischief. They cross to the teacher's desk, open it, look at the contents for a moment*]

ROCKY So what? Pens an' papers, big deal. We're allowed to look in here anyways.

[*Pause. He looks meaningfully to the filing cabinet*]

BINNIE Rocky ...
ROCKY Dare ya.
BINNIE Eee, Rockeee ...
ROCKY Dare ya!
BINNIE You couldn't get in there anyway.
ROCKY I bet I could.

[*He gives the drawer handle a casual yank; it slides open. Startled, he slams it shut*]

[*whispering a dirty secret*] 'S not even locked!

[*Pause. They stare at it, frightened*]

BINNIE Sometimes she leaves it unlocked. It's the honour system. She trusts us not to look.
ROCKY [*laughs*] Too bad for her, eh?
BINNIE That's not funny, Rocky! That stuff is top secret!
ROCKY Yeah, ya know why? Ya know what Mrs. Smith keeps in here?
BINNIE Yeah. They got files in there.
ROCKY Yeah. And those files say things about what's *wrong* with us. All our teachers decide whether they *like* us or not, by reading in here!
BINNIE It doesn't tell them to *like* us or not.
ROCKY It says whether we're gonna pass or flunk!
BINNIE So what?
ROCKY So I'm gonna open it.
BINNIE No! She could come in any minute.
ROCKY I thought she was s'posed to be havin' her baby.
BINNIE Well, Mr. Powers could come in. Anybody could come in.

[*They both look to the door for a paranoid moment*]

ROCKY Nah. I'm gonna do it.

[*He turns back with* BINNIE *to the filing cabinet. The door opens—on cue, as it were. We cannot yet see the intruder*]

I'm gonna open it.
BINNIE I'm not gonna watch.

[*She turns her back on* ROCKY, *and finds herself face to face with* VICTOR, *who has come in the door. He carries a tape recorder*]

ROCKY [*his attention on the filing cabinet*] 'Kay, here goes, I'm opening it now.
BINNIE Victor!

[ROCKY *whirls*]

VICTOR Hi, Binnie.
ROCKY Victor, Victor, Boa Constrictor. Whaddayou doin' here?
VICTOR I'm bringing a message from the Principal's Office.
ROCKY Why can't he bring his own messages?
VICTOR It's my job today. I'm the Day Monitor.
ROCKY [*playing deeply impressed*] Are ya!
BINNIE [*playing profound awe*] The real Day Monitor? Really? *Thee* Day Monitor?

[*She gets down on her knees and worships.* ROCKY *thinks this is quite funny*]

VICTOR All right, stop it.
ROCKY Hey, that's an important job, Day Vomiter.
VICTOR Monitor!
BINNIE That's what he said. Vomiter.
VICTOR No he didn't, he said 'vom'— Yeah, that's right. But it's 'monitor'!
BINNIE Oh! Well! I'm glad we got that straightened out, eh?

[*She and* ROCKY *do a poor job of stifling their amusement.* VICTOR *is not amused*]

VICTOR My message is, Mrs. Smith can't come today.

BINNIE What? I gotta show her my composition!
VICTOR She's in the hospital.
BINNIE Her baby! She's having her baby!
VICTOR Yeah, that was it.
BINNIE Yay, it's true, we were right, Mrs. Smith's having a little Smith!
VICTOR So anyway, today's class is cancelled. What were you two doing in here?
BINNIE Having a baby.
ROCKY Bin-*neee!!*
VICTOR Very funny.
ROCKY We were waiting for Mrs. Smith, 'cause we're s'posed to have—
BINNIE [*to* **ROCKY**] Don't tell him!
ROCKY Why not?
BINNIE [*to* **VICTOR**] None of your business what we're doing in here. This is our room. This is our special room for the special learning disabled kids and their special teacher who's having a baby—
VICTOR It's my business if you were trying to get into that filing cabinet.
BINNIE We were pretending! Is it open? We were pretending!
VICTOR Well, pretending or not, you might have had enough brains to lock the door.
ROCKY What?
VICTOR And leave the light off.
ROCKY Whaddayou mean, 'nough brains?
VICTOR Well, it kills me seeing guys like you trying to break the rules—
ROCKY 'Guys like you'—
VICTOR —and not even being able to do it right.

ROCKY You said I had no brains.
VICTOR Well, and all that hollering and screaming wasn't the smartest thing in the world either—

[ROCKY *spins the swivel chair* VICTOR *is sitting on*]

Stop it! Stop it! Don't hit me! Ow! Ow! Don't hit me!
ROCKY [*stops suddenly. Silence*] Whatcha scared of?
VICTOR Nothing.
ROCKY Scareda the dummy, Victor? Scareda the L-D?
VICTOR No.
ROCKY No? Oh. Then you must be ascareda the other L-D, you must be ascareda Binnie.
BINNIE Boo.
VICTOR I am not!
ROCKY Well, those're the only dummies here. Me and Binnie. Everybody else here's *real* smart.
VICTOR [*frightened*] I'm not scared of either of you. All I have to do is tell the Principal that—
ROCKY *Squealer!* Gonna tell him I gave you a little *push!*
VICTOR —that I heard you planning to break into the filing cabinet. [*brief pause*] I don't squeal for hitting. Guys hit me alla time, I don't tell. But getting into that thing is serious. That's school business. And I'm the Day Monitor.

[ROCKY *grabs* VICTOR*'s tape recorder*]

Doon't!
ROCKY You tell on us I'll break your tape recorder!
VICTOR You're too late! A bunch of Grade Sevens broke it this morning.

ROCKY [*turns the tape recorder on and shakes it*] Oh. Yeah. Nothin'.
VICTOR What do you wanna get in there for, anyway?
ROCKY I wanna find out if I'm flunking.
VICTOR Those files are just for the teachers.
BINNIE We know that. That's the problem! Don't you think it's weird how everybody's allowed to read them except—
VICTOR Aaghh! What're you doing!

[ROCKY *has delicately taken a strand of* VICTOR*'s hair*]

ROCKY Hold still. Don' move.
VICTOR What is it!
ROCKY Spider.
VICTOR Eeeuuuggghhh!
ROCKY Big one. Biig one.
VICTOR Take it out take it out take it out!

[ROCKY *pretends to remove it from* VICTOR*'s hair; meanwhile, he takes a toy rubber spider from his pocket*]

ROCKY I got it. It's still alive. I think it's a tarantula. You wanna see?
VICTOR No, thanks!
ROCKY [*shoving the rubber spider into* VICTOR*'s peripheral vision*] C'mon, it's big an' furry.
VICTOR No!
BINNIE Well, ya better hold still, it seems to like you. It keeps wiggling at you.

[ROCKY *backs up to the filing cabinet*]

VICTOR Don't let it near me.
BINNIE Inky dinky spider
   Got stepped on by a moose.
   Victor looked inside 'er:
   Eeuggh! Spider juice!
VICTOR Okay, Binnie, it's your fault if I throw up.
BINNIE [*to* ROCKY] Victor throws up easily.
ROCKY Yeah? That's 'cause he's the Day Vomiter, eh?

[*They laugh*]

Well, then, you don't wanna look at what I'm doing, Victor.
VICTOR I sure don't.

[ROCKY *opens the drawer. He peers in.* BINNIE *joins him, stifling her amusement—for it has now become a joke on* VICTOR*—and they gaze in at the files.* VICTOR *becomes suspicious and turns around*]

VICTOR Oooh, no you don't.
ROCKY [*wiggling the rubber spider in his direction*] Spider! Spider!
VICTOR No you don't. You don't fool me. Look what you did! You broke into the filing cabinet!
BINNIE We didn't break in, it wasn't even locked.

[*Hears herself rationalizing, exchanges guilty glance with* ROCKY]

ROCKY Whatcha gonna do about it, Victor?
VICTOR You'll see. You'll see. Just try taking those files

out of there, and you'll just see.

[*Beat.* ROCKY, *of course, starts taking the files out of the cabinet and looking at them. The file folders are of different colours, including red, blue, yellow and green*]

All right, wait a minute. Look. Uh—you're not gonna be able to understand these files, anyway, Rocky. These files are put together by experts, and—and, uh—

ROCKY [*continues looking through files, and tossing them on the floor*] So? I can try. You said I have no brains, but I know the difference between a rubber spider. I can try.

VICTOR Look. You want to find out if you're gonna pass? There's a really good way. It's called a report card. You ever heard of a report card? The reason for report cards is to tell you how you're doing, you know.

BINNIE Yeah, well, it's easy for you, you know. You always know how you're doing. You write those long book reports that're longer than the books, an' you're the teacher's pet an' everything, an' you get all A's!

VICTOR Well, I can't help it if I'm smart!

BINNIE [*doing her* VICTOR *imitation*] 'Well, I can't help it if I'm the biggest genius in the whole—'

VICTOR And I wouldn't if I could! 'Cause I am!

ROCKY What?

VICTOR Smart!

ROCKY Oh. Okay. So?

VICTOR So I may be a *nerd* and a *wimp* and everything, but at least I got one thing that's mine. I'm smarter than anybody else in this whole school. I know it may not be much, but it's mine!

ROCKY   Okay. Well. We're smarter'n you think we are, anyways.

VICTOR   Oh, yeah? And this is how you're showing it?

ROCKY   Maybe I'll show you when I find this dumb file. [*tosses files all over the floor, making quite a mess*]

VICTOR   Have you two gone crazy? This is serious! You could get expelled for this! You could get the strap!

BINNIE   Oh, Victor, they haven't had the strap for years.

VICTOR   Well, they should! For stuff like this! You have to go turn yourself in.

ROCKY   Whaddaya mean?

VICTOR   You have to go to the Principal's Office, and tell Mr. Powers what you did.

BINNIE   Are you crazy?

VICTOR   If you don't, you'll only get in worse trouble.

ROCKY   Only if you tell.

VICTOR   You're darn right I'm gonna tell! I have to tell!

ROCKY   [*making fists, threatening*] Then I have to smash your face in.

VICTOR   Rocky, I can't cover up for you.

ROCKY   Why not?

VICTOR   'Cause I'm the Day Vom—*Monitor!* I mean, look, you wouldn't cover up for me, would you? I *have* to tell the Principal! Or else *you* do.

ROCKY   I'm not tellin' no Principal!

VICTOR   [*though terrified*] Then I have to.

BINNIE   Wait. Wait. You guys calm down a second. Look. [*to* VICTOR] What if we just clean it all up an' put everything back exactly the way it was? So there won't be any harm done, right? So then you don't have to tell the Principal. [*to* ROCKY] And you won't have to smash his face in. 'Cause everything will be like it was, right?

NOT SO DUMB

VICTOR But everything *won't* be like it was, because Rocky's read his file! Or else he's gonna.
ROCKY I can't, dodo! You're tellin' me to turn myself in for readin' a file, an' I can't even read the file!
VICTOR You can't?
ROCKY I can't even find it.
VICTOR What? [*starts to laugh*] You broke into this thing just to look for a file you can't even read?
BINNIE It's not funny, Victor.
VICTOR [*laughing*] What a dummy! I've seen some dummies before, but you—you just—

[ROCKY *threatens him*]

Don't! Don't! Ow! Ow! Don't hit me! Don't hit me!
ROCKY Aaaaaaarrrrggghhhh!

[ROCKY *grabs* VICTOR'*s tape recorder, holds it up in the air, ready to smash it, possibly over* VICTOR'*s head.* BINNIE *gets on her hands and knees, bounds over to* ROCKY, *barking, and yanks his shoelaces undone with her teeth. Distracted, he turns and glares at her as she bounds back, still on hands and knees. She is imitating a large, sloppy dog*]

BINNIE Woof! Woof! Grrr-uff! [*sits up and pants*]
ROCKY Whaddayou doin'!
BINNIE I'm doing Snowy, my dog. Haven't you ever seen my Snowy imitation?
ROCKY Whatcha open my shoelaces for?
BINNIE To stop you beating up on Victor.
ROCKY Opening my shoelaces an' barking like your dog isn't gonna make me stop beating up on Victor!

BINNIE Well, it did …

[*Pause*]

ROCKY [*lamely*] Oh. Yeah. It did. [*beat*] Okay, Victor. Tie 'em back up, then.
VICTOR Me? She untied them!
ROCKY You started all this, you tie 'em up.
VICTOR What started all this was you not being able to read your files. I can't help it if it made me laugh.

[ROCKY *again wields the tape recorder*]

All right I'll do it don't hit me! [*kneels to tie the shoes*]
BINNIE Ya know the hardest thing about having a learning disability, Victor?
VICTOR What?
BINNIE Putting up with guys like you!
VICTOR Oh. Well. [*brief silence*] I'm sorry I laughed, okay?

[ROCKY *and* BINNIE *look at each other*]

BINNIE Okay.
ROCKY [*not angry*] Ya know somethin'? I wish it was you, Victor. Jus' for like one class, so you'd know what it's like. Sittin' in class and hoping she won't ask you. 'Cause ya know you'll do it wrong an' everybody'll laugh. Sometimes I see you get up to read or something, an' you do it so perfect, an' I just wish you knew what it was like to be me an' Binnie.
VICTOR [*finishes tying, stands*] Well, you know, everything

NOT SO DUMB

isn't exactly perfect for me either. Getting beaten up by guys at recess all the time—
BINNIE Well, at least you got all the grownups on your side. The teachers and stuff.
VICTOR Well, so what, when you don't have any friends?
ROCKY We don't have any friends either.
VICTOR Sure you do, you've got—never mind.
BINNIE You don't know what it's like, Victor. People calling you names all the time.
VICTOR Are you *kidding?* Are you *kidding?* I'm the world's greatest expert on being called names!
ROCKY Nobody ever called you stupid.
VICTOR No! Instead they call me a '*braaaayn*'!
ROCKY You know what they call me? A *ree*-tard.
VICTOR They call me a nerd.
ROCKY You called me a dummy!
VICTOR Oh yeah? Well, I'm a wimp!
ROCKY [*pointing to himself*] Feeb!
VICTOR [*ditto*] Weirdo!
ROCKY Idiot!
VICTOR *Four-Eyes!*
ROCKY *Moron!*
VICTOR *Egghead!*
ROCKY *Airhead!*
BINNIE Hold it!

[BINNIE *freezes.* ROCKY *and* VICTOR *freeze as well, in response to her*]

[*whispering*] Principal coming.

[*All remain frozen, listening. Then they all hear it. Immediate* action: BINNIE *and* ROCKY *dive behind the desk.* VICTOR *stands there for a moment, as if petrified with fear—but then he suddenly starts shouting]*

VICTOR Stupid! Brain! Retard! Nerd! Dummy! Wimp!

[*As he shouts, ignoring* ROCKY *and* BINNIE's *attempts to gesture him back to safety behind the desk, he quickly puts on two of the puppets: the Sponge Beast puppet and the Professor puppet, one on each hand. Then he opens the door*]

Feeb! Weirdo! Idiot! Four-Eyes! Moron! Egghead! Airhead— Oh, hi, Mr. Powers. [*pause*] Playing. [*pause*] Binnie and Rocky? They've left. [*pause*] Oh, that was me. This puppet is Binnie, and this puppet is, uh, Rocky. And I'm having a big fight between them. I'm releasing my feelings through creative play.

[*Pause, as Mr. Powers presumably absorbs this one*]

Oh. Okay. Bye, Mr. Powers.

[*Mr. Powers apparently leaves.* VICTOR *closes the door*]

We gotta be quieter, he's staying in his office for a while.

[ROCKY *slowly stands up from behind the desk, staring wildly at* VICTOR. *Slightly alarmed*]

I'm sorry. I wasn't out to make fun of you or anything. Don't hit me.

NOT SO DUMB

Stephen Aberle (VICTOR)

ROCKY   That was—that was great. That was absolutely fantastic!
BINNIE   [*getting up*] Not so dumb, Victor!
ROCKY   That was *fantastic!*

[VICTOR *blushes and shrugs*]

BINNIE   What didja tell him? Releasing your what?
VICTOR   'Releasing my feelings through creative play.' [*giggles*] I don't even know what it means. I read it in a book.
ROCKY   You read that? In a book?
VICTOR   A comic! I read it in a comic. Listen, we gotta clean up now.
ROCKY   Aw, *Victor—*

JOHN LAZARUS

VICTOR No, really! What if he comes back!
ROCKY [*alarmed, to* BINNIE] Hey, right.
BINNIE [*shrewdly*] Yeah, right, but then what? Ya still on him to turn himself in?
VICTOR Well, if he can't read his file, I guess there's nothing to tell the Principal.

[*Brief pause*]

ROCKY Well. Okay. Let's clean up.

[VICTOR *has put away the Sponge Beast but retained the Professor puppet. He sits admiring it, as* BINNIE *and* ROCKY *start work*]

BINNIE Victor, aren't you gonna help?
VICTOR [*as von Brainschtorm*] Ja! You vant me to help too?
ROCKY Oh, great. All we need.
VICTOR [*as von Brainschtorm*] Ja! You do need me! I am Doktor von Brainschtorm. I know all about important papers. Important papers are my beezness!
ROCKY Big deal.
VICTOR [*as von Brainschtorm*] Here, let me to be helpink mit zis. Vait chust a moment— [*takes some filing folders, tries to rearrange them. Puzzled, dropping the characterization*] Wait a second. These are all in different grades. And you've got them all mixed together.
BINNIE Oh, just put 'em away.
VICTOR But they have to go back in the same order, or she'll know.
BINNIE [*stops, looks*] Yeah, you're right.

VICTOR We have to go through every file and figure out what grade the kid is in! Oh, no, this is gonna take hours. [*opens one*] Well—I know this guy. He's in Grade Six.

BINNIE And this kid's in Grade Four.

VICTOR So's this one. Grade Four.

ROCKY That's why those are both yellow.

VICTOR Rocky, just— Here's another Grade Six.

ROCKY An' that one's green. Hey, wouldn't it be neat if that was how it worked? Green for Grade Six, yellow for Grade Four—

BINNIE Rocky, will you stop horsing around? Here's a Grade Five.

ROCKY An' then these other colours would all be for different grades. [*beat*] Wait a minute … [*suddenly starts re-checking the files*] Wait a minute. Wait a minute! I'm right! Yellow is Four, red is Five, green is Six and— Hey, look, you guys! Look!

BINNIE Rocky—

ROCKY I bet you blue is Grade Seven!

VICTOR Rocky, you're wasting time.

ROCKY I betcha! I betcha! Blue is Grade Seven!

BINNIE [*checks*] Hey, just a second. You know what, he's right!

VICTOR [*checks*] Hey, yeah! How'd you figure that out?

ROCKY 'Ts obvious.

VICTOR No it's not!

ROCKY 'Ts obvious to me.

[**ROCKY** *and* **VICTOR** *stare at each other for a moment*]

Okay, anyways, let's do it.

[ROCKY *grabs up a batch of yellow folders and shoves them into the filing cabinet drawer in random order*]

VICTOR Wait, you can't do it like that.
ROCKY Says who?
VICTOR Once the colours are together, they have to go in alphabetical order.
ROCKY Oh. [*to* BINNIE] Alphabetical order.
VICTOR So what's the problem?
ROCKY Nothin'.
VICTOR You don't know your alphabet?
ROCKY I know my alphabet! I just mix it up.
VICTOR What?
BINNIE He knows the letters, he just forgets what order they go in.
ROCKY Don' worry about it. You guys clean up. I'll watch.

[*He sits and watches, making a good effort not to be sullen.* BINNIE, *seeing* ROCKY'*s situation, grabs* VICTOR'*s tape recorder and hands it to* ROCKY]

BINNIE Hey Rock, see whatcha can do with this.
VICTOR Hey! Be careful with that!
BINNIE It's all right, just let him look at it, he won't hurt it. Eh, Rocky?
ROCKY [*already preoccupied with tape recorder*] Sure. [*takes a small screwdriver out of his pocket and starts digging away at it*]
VICTOR What're you doing to it?
ROCKY You'll get it back. [*opens the back of the tape recorder*]
VICTOR You give it back right now!

BINNIE Ten minutes, Victor. You'll get it back in ten minutes.
VICTOR In one piece! Just like it was!
ROCKY Maybe. Maybe not. We'll see.
VICTOR If I don't, you have to pay for it!
ROCKY It's a deal.

[*Beat*]

VICTOR Well, if you electrocute yourself, I'm not paying for the funeral.
ROCKY I'm taking out the batteries, I'm using a rubber-handled screwdriver, an' I'm sitting with my feet off the floor so I'm not even electrically grounded, 'kay?

[*Beat*]

VICTOR Guess so. I don't even know what you're talking about.
ROCKY Well, I do, an' it's safe.
BINNIE If Rocky says it's safe then it's safe, Victor.
VICTOR Wow. Okay.

[VICTOR *returns to picking up files.* BINNIE *joins in. So now we have* VICTOR *and* BINNIE *putting the files away, while* ROCKY *sits on a table or desk, fiddling with the guts of the dissected tape recorder*]

BINNIE [*as she cleans up*] Fudge, fudge,
Tell the judge,
Mrs. Smith's havin' a baby …
Pearl, pearl, it's a girl,

Mr. Smith's going crazy …
Wrap it up in tissue paper,
Send it up the elevator,
First floor, Stop—
Second floor, Stop—
VICTOR Binnie, stop it!
BINNIE Third floor, Stop—
Fourth floor, Stop—
Fifth floor, Stop—
Sixth floor, Stop—
ROCKY Bin-neee!
BINNIE Hey, ya know what we oughta do? We oughta put a big congratulations message on the blackboard for Mrs. Smith having her baby! Eh, Rocky?
ROCKY [*shrugs*] I don' care.
BINNIE You do it, Victor.
VICTOR [*preoccupied with files*] She's not my teacher.
ROCKY You do it, Bin.
BINNIE Yeah?
ROCKY Sure.
BINNIE All right!

[*Enthusiastically, she jumps up and begins to write on the blackboard. After a moment,* VICTOR *glances up, sees what she's writing, and freezes in amazement.* BINNIE *is writing the words 'Congratulations—Love, Binnie and Rocky' clearly, fluently, in respectable handwriting but backwards, in a mirror image*]

VICTOR How did you do that?
BINNIE What?
VICTOR How do you write like that? That is bizarre!

BINNIE Did I do it again? [*traces the letters with her finger*] Yeah. Did it again.
VICTOR You mean you can't even tell? If it's forward or backward?

[BINNIE, *embarrassed, doesn't answer*]

ROCKY Yeah, you gotta hold a mirror up to it, eh.
VICTOR [*hesitantly*] 'Con—gratulations—Love, Binnie and Rocky.'
ROCKY Don't put 'love'!
VICTOR Binnie, that is absolutely weird.
ROCKY Take out the 'love' part.
BINNIE Sure.

[BINNIE *erases the word 'love' and then continues, angrily rubbing out the rest of it*]

VICTOR [*blocks her from finishing*] No! Don't! Don't rub it all out! It's neat!
BINNIE It is not neat! It is backwards!
VICTOR I didn't know you were able to do this!
BINNIE I'm not able! I'm disabled! I can't tell the difference. I can't do it!
VICTOR Aw, you just don't try hard enough or something.
BINNIE *Try* hard enough? I work on it three hours a day! And half the weekend!
VICTOR *Why?*
BINNIE 'Cause I learn it upside down and inside out and backwards. The trouble is, they teach it right side up and forwards.
ROCKY Yeah!

Wendy Donaldson (BINNIE) and Thomas Hunt (ROCKY)

BINNIE Yeah! So don't gimme that about not trying hard enough, Victor!
VICTOR I think you guys are making up excuses.
BINNIE *Victorrr ...*

[**BINNIE** *tries to attack him.* **ROCKY** *intervenes*]

ROCKY Wait a minute! Wait a minute.

[**BINNIE** *holds off.* **ROCKY** *turns to* **VICTOR**]

Victor? You try it.
VICTOR Try what?
ROCKY Try writing like Binnie.
VICTOR Oh! Oh, sure.

[**VICTOR** *confidently crosses to the blackboard, tries to write 'Congratulations' in* **BINNIE**'s *mirror writing. Has trouble*]

Wait. No, wait a second.
ROCKY C'mon, Victor, you can do it. Maybe.
VICTOR Wait, no, the 'G' goes— This is trickier than it looks.
BINNIE You're just not trying hard enough, Victor!
VICTOR Quiet, you're distracting me!
ROCKY You're jus' making up excuses!
VICTOR How does— The letters won't go where I want!
ROCKY If you really wanted to, you could do it!
BINNIE Hurry up, the rest of the class is waiting!
VICTOR [*gives up*] All right! All right! I can't do it!

[**VICTOR** *throws the chalk down. Brief pause*]

ROCKY Well, the rest of us can do it, so what's wrong with you, Victor?
BINNIE Yeah, Victor, if you can't do better than that you'll flunk.
VICTOR I don't think that's very funny.
BINNIE Funny? No! No, it's not *funny!* This is how we feel all the time, Victor! Whenever we're trying to write forwards!
VICTOR But everybody's s'posed to write forwards. Writing forwards is normal!
ROCKY *Yeah!*

[*Pause*]

VICTOR [*still a bit puzzled*] Oh.
BINNIE So now you know, Victor.
ROCKY Maybe.

[ROCKY *returns to fiddling with the tape recorder.* BINNIE *returns to gathering up the last of the files.* VICTOR *picks up the two files he was looking at earlier*]

VICTOR You guys? I found your files.

[BINNIE *and* ROCKY *stop what they're doing and stare*]

'Garvey, Binnie.' And 'Keefer, Rupe—' uh, 'Rocky.'
BINNIE Look, never mind, just put 'em away in the drawer, okay?
VICTOR Don't you wanna read them?
ROCKY I can't read, an' she doesn't care. So you might as well put 'em away.

VICTOR Aren't you even gonna try?
BINNIE Victor …
VICTOR Well, you went to all this trouble and everything. You might as well just try.

[*Beat. Then* ROCKY *opens the file, shoves his face into it, closes it and hands it back*]

ROCKY There, I tried.
VICTOR You want me to read them?
BINNIE Let's not get in any more trouble.
VICTOR Hey, if I decide to read them, it isn't your fault, is it? Like if I read them out loud, and you two just happen to be sitting here in the room, well, you can't help that, can you?
ROCKY Aren't you afraid of getting in trouble?
VICTOR Yeah. But, like, what are friends for, anyway? Let me read you the files!

[*Pause.* BINNIE *and* ROCKY *do not answer. Nervously,* VICTOR *opens* BINNIE*'s file. He picks a sheet at random, and reads*]

VICTOR 'Binnie Garvey—Profile of Learning Disabilities: Temporal con—conceptualization, seven. Chronological ordination—' Weird stuff, eh? [*opens* ROCKY*'s file*] This is yours, Rocky. Same kind of stuff. Look at all these graphs and charts.
BINNIE No wonder she left it unlocked. We can't understand the junk anyways.
VICTOR Oh, here's some stuff they actually wrote in English. 'Rupert has dysleck—dyslex—'

ROCKY Dyslexia, dyscalculia, an' dysgraphia.

VICTOR [*checking that with the paper, impressed with* ROCKY's *knowledge*] Yeah! Right! Wow. 'But he's very bright: not only is he smarter than his fellow students think, he's even smarter than he thinks.'

ROCKY [*embarrassed*] Aw, that's stupid. Who wrote all this junk?

VICTOR [*leafing through the file*] Mrs. Morgan, Mr. Bakhtawar and Miss Chang.

BINNIE Your last three teachers! For the last three years!

ROCKY I told ya, this stuff follows you around. Listen, I've heard enough.

BINNIE Yeah, me too, we've heard enough, Victor.

VICTOR No, listen, this is interesting. Mrs. Smith wrote this part. 'His only close friend is—' [*stops, embarrassed*]

ROCKY Who? Who's my friend?

VICTOR 'Binnie Garvey, a learning-disabled girl who tries to hide her own problems by playing the class clown.'

[ROCKY *looks at* BINNIE, *who squirms.* VICTOR *continues, unaware*]

'He has a terrible temper. But this is because he wants so much to do well that he gets furious with himself. As far as we know he has never hurt a child, and probably never will.'

ROCKY All right, that's enough!

VICTOR 'Under his bullying exterior, Rocky is good, kind and loyal. If he can solve some of his problems, and I'm sure he will, he will turn out to be a splendid young man.'

ROCKY [*grabs the sheet from him*] I didn't ask ya to read this!

NOT SO DUMB

VICTOR What're you complaining about! She's saying terrific things here!
ROCKY I don't care! [*shoves him*] I never asked ya! [*shoves him again*]
VICTOR I just did it to be friendly! This is what I get for trying to help out!
BINNIE She got your name right, Rocky—
ROCKY [*getting close to him, making fists*] I oughta just—
VICTOR You don't scare me any more. 'Good, kind and loyal,' it says. 'Never hurt a kid and never will,' it says.

[*After a moment's internal struggle,* ROCKY *punches* VICTOR *in the biceps*]

Oooww! Oooowww! You hit me! You hit me!
ROCKY There. Now I hurt a kid. 'Kay?
VICTOR Binneeee! He hit meee!
BINNIE I think you asked for it, Victor.

[VICTOR *starts crying*]

ROCKY Hey, c'mon, I didn't hit ya that hard. [*to* BINNIE] Did I?
BINNIE Nah. That's just Victor. He's worse than my sister.
ROCKY Aw, Victor, c'mon, grow up, eh.
VICTOR Everybody always hits me! How come everybody's always hitting on mee!
ROCKY Don' take it personal, Victor. It's only 'cause you're a jerk.
VICTOR First you hit me, then you call me names!
ROCKY C'mon. Let's see what I did t'ya here. [*exposes bruise*]

VICTOR Ow.

ROCKY Hey, that's gonna be a good one. You should go home an' show this to your mom. Tell her you was in a fight, eh?

VICTOR [*sniff*] She'd have a raving cow fit.

BINNIE [*cheerfully*] Yeah …

ROCKY You can tell her you broke my nose or something. I don't care.

VICTOR [*sniff*] Really? Can I?

ROCKY Sure. Here, blow your nose. Here, uh—

[**ROCKY** *casts around, picks up a piece of paper, applies it to* **VICTOR**'s *nose*]

BINNIE Don't use that!

ROCKY Why not?

BINNIE 'Cause it's part of the files!

ROCKY It is? [*stifles a giggle*]

BINNIE I mean, really, *gross*.

VICTOR [*looks*] Yeah, it is, too. [*takes a closer look at the letter*] It's from Mrs. Smith to Mr. Powers.

BINNIE What's it say?

VICTOR 'Dear Frank'—that's Mr. Powers—'Now that I'm going to be off having my baby, I thought you'd find it acceptable if I don't come back for the rest of the year.'

ROCKY What? She's not coming back?

BINNIE She's not coming back?

ROCKY She can't not come back!

BINNIE I have to show her my composition!

ROCKY She's the only teacher who's ever helped me!

BINNIE What else does it say?

VICTOR 'Jack and I have discussed this—'
BINNIE That's her husband that's her husband!
VICTOR Do you want to hear this or not?
BINNIE [*overexcited*] I'm just telling you, that's her husband!
ROCKY Will you be quiet an' pay attention!
BINNIE Sorree ... [*crosses, sits away from the boys, sulks*]
VICTOR 'Jack and I have discussed this, and I want to spend the next few years at home with my child. When she gets a bit older, I hope to return to teaching learning-disabled kids. I'm going to miss them, but I've had to decide my baby comes first for now.'
ROCKY She can't not come back! She can't!

[*No response from* BINNIE *and* VICTOR]

She can't! [*runs out the door*]
VICTOR Rocky— [*to* BINNIE] Where's he going?
BINNIE [*face hidden*] Who cares?
VICTOR Are you crying? What're you crying for?
BINNIE Who cares?
VICTOR Well, stop it, it makes you look silly.
BINNIE Who cares if I look silly? I'm gonna flunk now.
VICTOR What? No you're not.
BINNIE Whaddayou care, anyway? How'm I s'posed to pass when I'm writing backwards alla time? Mrs. Smith's the only one who could help me from flunking. An' now she's gone, and everybody'll think I'm stupid again, an' who cares, anyway?

[BINNIE *cries. Pause*]

VICTOR Aw, come on, she cares. But she has to take care

of her baby, you don't want her not to take care of her baby, do you?

BINNIE [*miserable, folded up in fetal position*] I dunno. I'm being punished for looking in the filing cabinet, that's what it is.

VICTOR Oh, come on, lots of people care!

BINNIE Lea' me alone, Victor!

[*Pause.* VICTOR *looks about, somewhat at a loss. Then he picks up the Doktor von Brainschtorm puppet. Puts it on. Approaches* BINNIE *with it*]

VICTOR [*as von Brainschtorm*] Vat's de matter, little Binschki?

BINNIE I said, leave me alone, Victor.

VICTOR [*as von Brainschtorm*] I am not Wiktor, I am Doktor von Brainschtorm. You know vat? I saw you dancink zis morning at recess. You're pretty good, you know. I can dance too, you know! You vant to see me?

BINNIE No.

VICTOR [*as von Brainschtorm*] Oh, come on, I'm really good. Come on, let me show you.

BINNIE You can't dance, 'cause you don't have any feet. Oh, great, now I'm talkin' to a puppet.

VICTOR [*as von Brainschtorm*] Look, I'm goink to do it now! You're goink to miss it! A-vun, two, tree, four—

[BINNIE *resignedly looks.* VICTOR *makes von Brainschtorm dance in the latest style, while singing, in his German accent, a current pop hit*]

BINNIE That's okay, I guess.

VICTOR [*as von Brainschtorm*] Sank you. I am glad you are likink it.

BINNIE [*reluctantly cheering up*] I didn't say I *liked* it. I said it was *okay*.

VICTOR Thanks.

[ROCKY *enters*]

Where were you?

ROCKY Principal's Office. I told Mr. Powers.

VICTOR What! What did you tell him!

ROCKY I told him I opened the filing cabinet, an' I read part of my file, and I couldn't understand most of it.

BINNIE What'd he say!

ROCKY He said to come into the office tomorrow an' see him.

VICTOR What's he gonna do to you!

ROCKY Well—it's weird. He's gonna tell my parents, but he said he's gonna explain why I did it. An' then I gotta go to his office every day after school for the next week—

BINNIE Uh oh.

ROCKY Yeah, I gotta do extra work an' stuff. But also, he said he'd explain my file to me. He wasn't really so mad. He said the files aren't supposed to be such a big secret. It's just confidential so everybody else can't see 'em all the time. An' guess what? He wants to work with me on some of the stuff Mrs. Smith does.

BINNIE You? What about me?

ROCKY Oh. I dunno. I guess it means you too.

BINNIE I could go ask him—

VICTOR Wait a minute. What'd you tell him about us?

JOHN LAZARUS

About us helping you?
ROCKY Nothin'! I'm no squealer!
VICTOR Oh, good.
ROCKY Anyways, I didn't have to tell him anything. He knew we were all here. That puppet stuff you did, you know, that didn't fool him for a second, he says.
VICTOR [*saving face*] Oh. Well—the Principal's supposed to be smarter than the kids, it's part of his job.
BINNIE That means he knows I helped open the filing cabinet.
VICTOR And me.
BINNIE So why doesn't he come after us?
ROCKY Maybe he's waitin'.

[*Pause.* BINNIE *looks to* VICTOR]

VICTOR Well—uh—if you wanna go ask him to help you like he's gonna help Rocky—
BINNIE Then I have to say I opened the files.
VICTOR And I guess I have to too. Uh—it might be easier if you came with us, Rocky.
ROCKY Sure. I'll protect you, Victor.
VICTOR Oh, great.
BINNIE Let's go! No, wait a sec!

[*She goes to the blackboard, and fills in the erased part of her message to Mrs. Smith again—still in mirror writing*]

ROCKY What's it say now?
BINNIE Same thing. 'Congratulations—Love, Rocky and Binnie.' 'Kay?
ROCKY [*totally casual*] 'Kay.

105

VICTOR I'm nervous about going.
ROCKY Aw, don't be nervous. Just be your usual nerdy self an' he'll think you're great.
VICTOR Hey, look. I won't call you a dummy, and you don't call me a nerd. Deal?

[*Beat*]

ROCKY Deal.
BINNIE Here, don't forget your tape recorder. [*hands the tape recorder, again in one piece, to* VICTOR]
VICTOR Oh, yeah, thanks.
ROCKY [*grinning*] Arencha gonna turn it on?

[VICTOR *resignedly turns it on. The latest heavy metal group (so up-to-date that even the author has never heard of it) comes roaring out of the tape recorder at top volume, sounding great.* VICTOR *stands staring open-mouthed at* ROCKY, *who can't help preening a little*]

VICTOR You fixed it! You fixed it! You fixed a whole tape recorder!
ROCKY Yeah.
VICTOR Not so dumb, Rocky!
BINNIE All right! Come on!

[BINNIE *sings with the music as she starts to dance out the door. The other two follow her*]

NIGHT LIGHT

Production History

Night Light was first produced by Green Thumb Theatre for Young People, at Henry Hudson Elementary School, Vancouver, on September 18, 1986, with the following cast:

FARLEY / MONSTER, Brent Applegath
VICTOR, Stephen Aberle
TARA, Carolyn Soper

Director: Dennis Foon
Set and Costume Designer: Marti Wright
Stage Manager: Susan Loadman
Monster Design and Construction: Lorraine Konst

Subsequently it received three more productions by Green Thumb, and productions by Actors Showcase (Winnipeg), Grand Theatre (London, Ontario), Magnus Theatre Lab (Thunder Bay), Chinook Theatre (Edmonton), Globe Theatre (Regina) and George Street Playhouse (New Jersey). *Night Light* has received a Jessie Award.

Acknowledgements

My thanks to Dennis, for help on developing the play from the very beginning; to the casts and stage managers of the first two productions, as well as guest observer Anne Hines, for their many crucial contributions to the script; to Elizabeth Dancoes, who helped workshop an earlier draft; to Green Thumb Theatre generally, for everything; and to Marietta Kozak for everything else.

Some of the techniques described herein are taken from a fine book called *Helping the Fearful Child*, by Jonathan Kellerman (New York: W.W. Norton, 1981).

And finally, my thanks to my mother, Selma Lazarus, for useful information on how she handled my own childhood fears. This play is dedicated to her.

Characters

VICTOR Ten. This is the **VICTOR** of *Not So Dumb*, some time later.

FARLEY Ten.

TARA **VICTOR**'s younger sister, about seven.

MONSTER a green, reptilian, one-eyed creature that emerges from the top of **TARA**'s bedroom dresser when she is frightened. Manipulated by the actor who plays **FARLEY**.

Setting

Two settings: the schoolyard during the day, and TARA's bedroom at night.

The schoolyard setting involves a chain-link fence (ideally a real one), and a sort of jungle-gym affair for the characters to climb on.

The bedroom includes TARA's bed, and a dresser which has practical drawers, but which also has the magical capability of allowing the MONSTER to arise out of its top and to have the MONSTER's claws come grasping up out of its drawers.

Schoolyard

Enter **FARLEY**, *bouncing a soccer ball and carrying a sheet of paper: his Socials exam*

FARLEY Six out of ten. What kind of a dumb mark is six outa ten. Dad's gonna kill me. Again.

[*He crumples the exam, throws it away. Starts to leave, pauses, retrieves the exam paper, de-crumples it*]

Well, it's better than the three outa ten I got last time. Yeah, but he won't care. 'It's gotta be at least an eight or it doesn't count.' Gee, that six almost looks like an eight. [*looks around him. The coast is clear. Takes out pencil*] He never checks the questions anyway, he only looks at the mark.

[**FARLEY** *forges an '8' over the '6'. Enter* **VICTOR**, *reading a book.* **FARLEY** *pockets the exam paper, blocks* **VICTOR**'s *way*]

Hey, Victor.
VICTOR [*not pleased*] Hi, Farley.
FARLEY Where you going? You going home, Victor?
VICTOR Leave me alone, Farley.
FARLEY Whatcha get on the Socials test?
VICTOR None of your business.
FARLEY Get an eight?

VICTOR None of your business.

[**FARLEY** *grabs* **VICTOR**'s *backpack, runs up the jungle gym with it*]

Gimme back my backpack!
FARLEY No.
VICTOR Farley—
FARLEY [*pulls out book*] What's this, Victor?
VICTOR It's my Science book. Give it back.

[**FARLEY** *tosses it over* **VICTOR**'s *head, so that it hits the ground, and resumes rummaging in the backpack*]

FARLEY Say Victor is a nerd.

[**FARLEY** *tosses another book: same result*]

VICTOR No.
FARLEY Say it.

[*He tosses another book; continues scattering* **VICTOR**'s *books*]

VICTOR If I say it, will you give me my backpack back?
FARLEY Maybe.
VICTOR [*inaudibly*] Victor is a nerd.
FARLEY Say it again, louder.
VICTOR Victor is a nerd.

[*By now* **VICTOR** *has gathered up his books.* **FARLEY** *tosses one more*]

TARA [*entering*] Victor!

[VICTOR *grabs for the last book, and all the others fall to the floor*]

Whatcha doing?
VICTOR Nothing. Go away.
TARA Why are your books on the ground?
VICTOR Tara, Mummy wants you at home.
TARA She does not.
VICTOR Well, go home anyways.
TARA Is Farley picking on you again?
VICTOR No. We're playing.
TARA Why don't you get your backpack back?
FARLEY Yeah, Victor, come and get it.
TARA Get him, Victor, come on. [*starts pushing* VICTOR *towards the jungle gym*]
VICTOR Will you be quiet?
TARA Kill 'im, Victor, go for it!
VICTOR Tara, I don't want to hurt him.
FARLEY Come on, Victor. Make my day.
VICTOR Farley, leave me alone— Don't hit me! Don't hit me!

[FARLEY *jumps off the jungle gym, attacks* VICTOR, *pins his arm behind him*]

TARA Come on, Victor, you're bigger than him. Get him!
VICTOR [*pinned; to* TARA] Pleeeze go home!
TARA You're a wimp, Victor. [*exit*]
FARLEY [*letting go*] Ha! Even your little sister knows you're a wimp.

VICTOR You know, it just so happens that our father happens to have gone into the hospital today, and you shouldn't—
FARLEY Aaaawww. Aaaawww. Is Daddy in the hospital?
VICTOR Knock it off!
FARLEY Or what, chicken?
VICTOR Nothing, nothing, don't hit me.

[VICTOR *resumes gathering books.* FARLEY *sits and watches. Brief silence*]

FARLEY So whadidja get on the Socials test?
VICTOR I did okay.
FARLEY Tell me. Whadidja get? Ja get an eight?
VICTOR I did okay.
FARLEY You wanna know what I got?
VICTOR To be quite frank, I don't care.
FARLEY Quite Frank? Whaddaya mean you don't care, Quite Frank?
VICTOR All right, what did you get?
FARLEY I got an eight out of ten. [*shows him the exam*]
VICTOR That's not an eight. It's a six that's been changed to look like an eight.
FARLEY What did you get? I told you what I got. You tell me what you got or I'll knock your teeth in.
VICTOR I got a ten.
FARLEY Ten?
VICTOR I'm sorry.
FARLEY Well, you know what? Since you're so smart? You know what you can do? [*shoves a notebook at him*] You can do my Math homework tonight. Or else.
VICTOR Okay.

JOHN LAZARUS

FARLEY And since you got a ten in the Socials, that means you'll get perfect on the Math. Right?
VICTOR Just 'cause I got a ten on one thing doesn't mean I'll get a—
FARLEY You better. You just better. I expect a perfect mark. I always expect the best from you, Victor. Victor, Victor, Boa Constrictor. Hah! [*exit*]

[VICTOR *picks up his books and exits*]

Bedroom

Enter TARA, *ready for bed, carrying her favourite doll, a stuffed cloth robot named Kosmo*

TARA Okay, Kosmo. See anything? Let's just look around. Under here, okay? [*sticks Kosmo's head under a pile of clothes so that the doll can 'look'*] All clear? Good. Now you check in the drawers, okay? [*pokes Kosmo's head into the dresser drawers*] All clear? Good. [*stands by the dresser, a short distance from the bed*] Now the leap. Ready? [*leaps onto the bed. Stamps on the bed to scare away anything beneath*] Hear anything? Good. Okay, now you look under the bed. Go! [*shoves Kosmo under the bed*] All clear? Lemme double-check. [*looks under the bed, yelps, pulls back. Looks again. Finds a Teddy bear, pulls it out*] Silly Kosmo! It was only Irving the Bear. Now don't be scared, Kosmo. There's nothing to be scared of, so you just go straight to sleep. They're not gonna hurt Daddy in the hospital. They're just gonna stick a needle in him to make him sleep, an' then they'll cut him open and stick more needles and threads in him, so there's nothing to worry about, okay? [*climbs into bed; watches dresser*] So you just shut your eyes and go to sleep. No staring around the room, trying to scare yourself, okay? 'Cause there's no Monster, okay? Don't be scared, there's no great big gross ugly Monster, watching you—waiting for you to go to sleep so it can come down on the bed an' bite you open and stick needles and threads in you—

[*One* MONSTER *hand begins to emerge out of a dresser drawer*]

Mum-meee ...

[*The other* MONSTER *hand emerges over top of the dresser*]

Mummeee!
VICTOR [*enters*] Will you be quiet?
TARA Look! Look at the dresser! There's a Monster! Its hands are sticking out!
VICTOR There's nothing! There isn't anything there, Tara.
TARA What?
VICTOR There is no Monster in your dresser, okay? Gimme a break, don't pull this stuff tonight.

[*The* MONSTER'*s hands fade back into the dresser*]

First you get Farley beating me up this afternoon, thank you very much, so now I have to do Farley's homework on top of my own homework—and now you're giving me monsters.

TARA I don't care, there was a Monster! There was!

VICTOR And Mummy is trying to take a nap. She had a long hard day, all right? She had to drive Daddy to the hospital and everything.

TARA I know that.

VICTOR Other people in this house are having problems, all right? Other people are scared too, all right? So quiet down and go to sleep. [*starts to exit*]

TARA Don't go away, it might come back!

VICTOR Aw, Tara—

TARA Can I go climb into bed with Mummy? I won't wake her up.

VICTOR Oh, sure you won't. Anyway, remember the new rule? No climbing into bed with Mummy and Daddy any more.

TARA Daddy's not here.

VICTOR Well, so what? What do you want me to do about it?

TARA I want a night light.

VICTOR A night light?

TARA Yeah.

VICTOR You're too old for a night light.

TARA No I'm not. Mummy told me Daddy has one in the hospital. They have them for everybody there. Grownups and everybody.

VICTOR Those are for calling the nurse.

TARA The nurse? What do they have to call the nurse for? You mean if their insides are falling out?

VICTOR What? Daddy's insides are not gonna fall out! It's just a hernia operation. To keep his insides from falling out.

TARA [*newly worried*] It is?

NIGHT LIGHT

VICTOR It's a simple, routine operation, they do them all the time. Things nev—hardly ever go wrong.
TARA Hardly ever? Whaddaya mean, hardly ever?
VICTOR Nothing. Never mind. Things never go wrong, okay? Just drop it, okay?
TARA But what if he has the operation, and then he wakes up and it's all dark and there might be monsters—or what if they missed a stitch and his insides are falling out?

[*As she has been speaking, the* **MONSTER** *hands have reappeared out of the dresser. Now she screams*]

It's back! It's back! Look out!
VICTOR What?
TARA The monster's back in the dresser!
VICTOR What's the matter with you, anyway, you're afraid of a dresser? It's just a dresser full of clothes.

[**VICTOR** *pulls a shirt out of the dresser. The* **MONSTER** *hands are grabbing at him, but he does not notice*]

TARA Dooon't!
VICTOR [*leans over the dresser, the* **MONSTER**'*s hands groping him*] Look. There's nothing here. See? All there is is drawers with some clothes in it. Shirts, shorts, underwear ....
TARA Victor, look out, it's grabbing you!
VICTOR [*his head virtually hidden by the* **MONSTER** *hands enveloping him and mushing him about*] Eeugghh. Tara, how many times does Mummy have to tell you not to put your dirty socks back in the dresser—

TARA Victor, don't you even see it? Can't you feel it on you?
VICTOR [*mockingly throws a sock at her*] Tara, you're such a wimp. Such a chicken.
TARA [*angry now*] Oooh! You sound just like Farley.

[TARA *throws the sock back at him. The* MONSTER *hands, alarmed by her anger, pull back into the dresser*]

Hey. It's gone.
VICTOR Okay. So are you okay, or what? You gonna go to sleep so I can go do Farley's Math?
TARA Hypnotize me?
VICTOR Hypnotize you?
TARA Please?

[VICTOR *takes a garment and slings it over his shoulders as a cape. Tears his Velcroed watch from his wrist and uses it to make hypnotic passes. Fake European accent, as he backs towards the door*]

VICTOR You are getteeng drowwwsy. Your eyeleeds are all getteeng heavvveee …

[*Etc., ad lib, until* TARA *yawns and settles down with Kosmo.* VICTOR *takes off the garment, leaves it on top of the dresser and exits.* TARA *opens her eyes long enough to see the* MONSTER'*s hand emerge and pull the garment back into the drawer. She yanks the bedclothes over her head*]

NIGHT LIGHT

Schoolyard

FARLEY *and* VICTOR, FARLEY *using his soccer ball as a threat or a weapon*

FARLEY Hey. You're in real trouble.

VICTOR What? Why? Whaddaya want from me? I been doing your Math homework every night.

FARLEY Yeah. An' now there's a big test coming up, an' I'm not ready.

VICTOR That isn't my fault.

FARLEY Well, you gotta sit next to me.

VICTOR What?

FARLEY You gotta ask Miss Donaldson to move your seat. So I can look over your shoulder in the test.

VICTOR I'm not gonna cheat.

FARLEY 'I'm not gonna cheat.' You think you're so smart you never have to cheat or anything.

VICTOR It has nothing to do with—

FARLEY You're not so smart, you know, Victor. When my father was in school, he was so smart he skipped Grade Six Math.

VICTOR Your father's smart?

FARLEY Whaddaya so surprised?

VICTOR Um, I'm not surprised, I just—

FARLEY He's a mining engineer. He works with big computers. Hundreds of people's lives depend on how smart my father is. He can do long division in his head. Can you do long division in your head?

VICTOR No.

FARLEY I can't even do long division on paper an' he can do it in his head, that's how smart he is.

VICTOR Well, that's, uh, that's great, Farley.
FARLEY Whaddaya mean, it's great? It stinks. I'm gonna flunk this test. So you gotta sit next to me.
VICTOR I'm not gonna cheat. And you don't have to flunk. Listen—
FARLEY Are you kidding? It's whole numbers an' decimal fractions. Decimal fractions. I got enough trouble with real fractions.
VICTOR Decimal fractions are real fractions. A decimal just means a tenth.
FARLEY Button your face! Who asked you?
VICTOR But it's easy! It's just like dollars and cents. You know how a dollar is—

[FARLEY *knocks* VICTOR's *book to the ground*]

Hey! What's that for?
FARLEY I just want ya to sit next to me on the test. Not to coach me. I don't need your crummy help. [*picks up* VICTOR's *book, keeps it from him*] I don't need your crummy books an'— [FARLEY *stops, stares at the book*] What the heck is this? *Mommy, I'm Scared: A Book on Children's Fears.*
VICTOR Farley—
FARLEY What a stupid book. 'Mommy, I'm so scared!' 'Mommy, I'm so scaaared!'
VICTOR It's for Tara. I told you, my father's in the hospital.
FARLEY 'Oooh, Mommy, I'm so scared, is Daddy gonna drop dead and never kiss me any more?'
VICTOR [*loses temper*] You don't understand anything!

[VICTOR *aggressively grabs book.* FARLEY *shoves his soccer*

NIGHT LIGHT

ball into VICTOR's *stomach, winding him.* VICTOR *doubles over*]

FARLEY 'Mommy, I'm so scared ...' Victor, I'm so scared.

[FARLEY *grabs back soccer ball, slams book into* VICTOR's *stomach in its place. Exit, leaving* VICTOR *catching his breath*]

[*chants*] Victor, I'm so sca-ared— Victor, I'm so scaared ...

[VICTOR *slowly gets up and exits*]

Bedroom

TARA *and* VICTOR *come into the bedroom,* TARA *carrying Kosmo*

TARA Yay, Victor! I love presents.
VICTOR Well, this isn't anything really special. I found it in the basement for you.
TARA What?
VICTOR [*producing night light*] Ta-daaahh!
TARA What is it?
VICTOR It's your night light!
TARA It's got a Snooky Bunny on it. Oh, Victor, Snooky Bunny is for babies.
VICTOR Hey, thanks, this used to be my Snooky Bunny.
TARA You had a Snooky Bunny night light?
VICTOR [*trying to get night light to work*] When I was really little. Don't tell anybody. Especially not Farley. Oh, phooey, it doesn't work. Tell you what, though,

I'll bring it over to Rocky's tomorrow. He'll fix it, he can fix anything.

TARA Daddy can fix it too. He can fix it when he comes home tonight.

VICTOR Uh, no. Mummy phoned while you were taking your bath—

TARA Yeah, an' I'm allowed to stay up and see Daddy all better when he gets home.

VICTOR No, Mummy says the doctor says he isn't coming home for a couple of days.

TARA What? He's s'posed to be home tonight, the operation's over!

VICTOR Well, nobody said tonight for sure. They thought probably tonight. If everything went fine.

TARA Something went wrong. You told me nothing ever goes wrong.

VICTOR Nothing went wrong!

TARA Liar!

VICTOR He's fine, the operation went perfectly. He just has a little temperature. Sometimes that means there's germs, where they cut him open.

TARA You mean he could die?

VICTOR No.

TARA Victor? Is he gonna die?

VICTOR No, he's not gonna die! If there's germs they get rid of them and he'll be fine. He'll be fine. It's nothing. Honest. He'll be home in a couple of days. I'll get this fixed and you'll have it tomorrow, okay? I promise. I have to go do my homework.

[*Exit.* TARA *is left sitting alone on the bed. She lies down and tries to prepare for sleep*]

TARA He'll be fine, Kosmo. It's nothing. He'll be home soon. They'll get rid of these germs that got in there. He's just a tiny bit sick—'cause those germs are growing, that's all—growing an' growing an' growing—an' climbing up out of the place where they cut him open—

[*As she speaks, the* MONSTER *rises up out of the dresser, its eye closed*]

Kosmo! There it is again! An' it looks like a germ!

[*The* MONSTER *opens its eye.* TARA *screams*]

Victorrr! Victorrr!

MONSTER Grrrr.

TARA [*screams*] Victor the Monster's here an' it's staring at me I'm scared Daddy help me I'm scared Victor I'm scaaaared!

VICTOR [*runs in, carrying the* Mommy *book*] Tara, for Pete's sake will you be quiet?

TARA There! On the dresser! The Monster!

VICTOR Oh, it's those stupid hands again?

TARA It isn't just hands this time, there's a whole face!

VICTOR [*staring straight at the* MONSTER, *who cheerfully stares back*] Tara, you know there isn't really a Monster there, don't you?

TARA Yes there is so!

VICTOR There is not, there's nothing there.

TARA It's right in front of you! It's staring you right in the face!

VICTOR [*nose to nose, eye to eye, practically touching*] Well, I don't see anything.

TARA Well, I do!
MONSTER Grrrr.
TARA What am I gonna dooo?
VICTOR All right, look, don't start wailing. I got this book out of the library—
TARA Aw, Victor, I don't want some dumb book.
VICTOR It's about what to do when you're scared. You wanna know how to keep the Monster from hurting you?
TARA Yeah.
VICTOR It says you should draw pictures of the Monster.
MONSTER [*approvingly*] Mmmm.
TARA Pictures? Why?
VICTOR I don't know.
TARA Okay.
VICTOR Okay. So, uh, what colour is it?
TARA [*takes papers and felts, spreads them out, starts drawing*] It's kind of an ugly greeny browny colour.
MONSTER Hmph.
VICTOR [*looking over her shoulder*] Yeah? Okay. Uh, what's its skin like?
TARA It's all scabby, wrinkly, lumpy an' very gross.
MONSTER Ahhhh.
VICTOR Eugh. So, uh, what colour eyes?
TARA It only has one eye. In the middle.

[MONSTER *bats its eyelashes*]

VICTOR Really? That is bizarre. What colour?
TARA It's got all red streaks in the white part, and it's sort of green but mostly black, and it has thick eyelashes.

[MONSTER *bats its eyelashes*]

VICTOR Does it have a mouth?
TARA It has a red mouth an' big white teeth.
MONSTER [*shows its teeth*] Grrrrr.
TARA Oh, Victor, it's growling and showing its teeth what do I do!
VICTOR Um, uh—draw them.
TARA Draw the teeth?
VICTOR Yeah.
TARA 'Cause maybe it's showing its teeth 'cause it wants me to draw them?
VICTOR I dunno.
TARA [*drawing*] Okay.
MONSTER [*batting eyelashes*] Purrrr.
VICTOR Stopped growling?
TARA Yeah.
VICTOR Good. [*admiring picture*] Hey, that's pretty good.
TARA No it isn't. It's yucky, 'cause the Monster's yucky.
MONSTER Grrr.
VICTOR Is it finished?
TARA Yeah.
VICTOR Right. So now you tear it up.
TARA What?
MONSTER Huh?
VICTOR That's what it says in the book. It says now you're s'posed to get mad at the Monster and tear up the picture.
MONSTER Hmph!
VICTOR 'Cause the book says you can't be mad and scared at the same time. So if you get mad at it and tear it up, you won't be as afraid of it. So go ahead, tear it up.
MONSTER Grrrr.
TARA I can't!

VICTOR Yes, you can. Slap it around.

[*She slaps at the picture. The* **MONSTER** *reacts as if slapped*]

MONSTER Grrraaarrgh!
VICTOR Punch it in the mouth!

[**TARA** *punches the* **MONSTER**'s *picture. The* **MONSTER** *reacts*]

Poke it in the eye!

[**TARA** *stabs the picture with a pen; the* **MONSTER** *reacts, putting a hand over its eye*]

Now: rip it up!
TARA [*doing so*] You mean bad Monster I'm gonna tear you up an' rip you up an' tear you into a million billion trillion pieces until you are dead and gone and far away forever!

[*As she does this, the* **MONSTER** *feels the tearing personally. Torn and flayed and in pain, it sinks into the dresser and is gone. Pause at the end of all this, with torn pieces of paper fluttering down and* **TARA** *catching her breath*]

VICTOR All right. That was neat. So what happened to the Monster?
TARA [*looks*] It's gone.
VICTOR Really?
TARA Well, it might be hiding in the dresser. You go check.
VICTOR Okay, I'll check. [*crosses to the dresser, rummages*

NIGHT LIGHT

about in the drawers] Is it getting its hands all over me like last time?
TARA No.
VICTOR Come and see. Come on.

[TARA *gets up and crosses hesitantly, hanging onto Kosmo*]

VICTOR [*head and arms in dresser drawer*] Uh oh— Oh, no—
TARA What? Victor, what?

[*A hand comes up out of the drawer and grabs* VICTOR *by the throat. He makes loud choking sounds*]

VICTOR Grrraaarrr! Glllgggkkk! Help! Help!

[TARA *begins shouting.* VICTOR *stands up away from the dresser, revealing that the hand is his own. He starts to laugh*]

TARA Oh, very funny, Victor.

[*But this amuses and emboldens her. She crosses to the dresser and looks inside, but is still tentative about reaching in*]

No Monster.
VICTOR No Monster. It worked. Jeez, I didn't think it would actually work.
TARA Now you gotta do Farley. You gotta draw a picture of Farley an' tear it up.
VICTOR [*takes a handful of torn paper from his pocket, tosses it*] I already did.

TARA [*laughs*] All right, Victor! So now Farley's dead an' gone forever too, eh?

VICTOR No, I think this only works on monsters. Farley'll be there tomorrow like always, waiting in the schoolyard with his stupid soccer ball. Tearing up paper isn't any good with Farley. Nothing's any good with Farley.

TARA Doesn't the book have anything else?

VICTOR Oh, it has this whole chapter on bullies, but it's kind of dumb. It says bullies are more scared than anybody. More scared than the people they're beating up on. Doesn't make any sense.

TARA But does it tell you what to do?

VICTOR It has this weird thing called 'The Scientist and Monkey Technique.' I'm s'posed to pretend I'm a scientist and Farley is a monkey.

TARA That'd be easy with Farley.

VICTOR Yeah, he's got the face, eh.

TARA Try it on me. Try it on me.

VICTOR Oh, it's silly.

TARA Aw, come on. I'll be Farley. Please?

VICTOR Oh, all right. You be Farley and I'll be me. I'm walking through the schoolyard and you stop me.

TARA [*as* FARLEY, *stands up on bed to be level with him*] Hey, Victor, Victor, Bow Kastickter. You're a nerd.

VICTOR [*checks his watch, makes notes*] Okay, it's eight fourteen and thirty-two seconds and I'm a nerd. Thank you, Farley.

TARA Ooh, Nerd Face, what're ya doing, extra homework for the teacher?

VICTOR That's very good, Farley. Extra homework for the teacher ... Seven seconds.

TARA [*jumps on* VICTOR's *back, rides him around*] If you don't put that pen down, I'm gonna beat you up and knock your head off and punch you in the stomach and trip you up and pull your hair and put my hand down your throat and pull out your tonsils!

VICTOR [*still making notes with* TARA *on his shoulders*] Gonna beat me up and knock my head off and pull my hair and trip me up and—pull out my tonsils?

TARA [*slides off him to the floor*] Yeah, you're right, Victor, this is no fun.

VICTOR [*alert*] What do you mean? What do you mean, no fun?

TARA It's boring.

VICTOR Yeah? Really? Are you bored?

TARA Well, sure. I just keep saying mean things and you don't get mad or scared or anything, it's really stupid.

VICTOR Yeah! Yeah! That's the whole idea. [*gathers up notebook, pencil, etc.*] That's what'll happen to Farley, I'll do this and he'll get fed up and then he'll leave me alone. This is great! This is gonna work! [*runs out*]

TARA Victor— No, Victor, wait! [*grabs Kosmo, runs out after him*]

Schoolyard

Enter FARLEY *as a semi-robot, with a bag of chips*

FARLEY Here's Farley, the famous computerized robot, looking for evildoers and scum. My genius father put a computer inside my head, and made my body bullet-proof. So now I can figure out everything, and get shot without feeling it, and see around corners, and— [*sees bad guys. Emits computer noises. In robot monotone*] You have three seconds to surrender, Slime Face …

[FARLEY *is shot, but unhurt by bullets. Shoots, including behind his head. Twirls and replaces gun*]

[*back to normal voice*] And so I'm the perfect defender machine! But now my father is being held prisoner by terrible bad guys. And I can't figure out where they are. So I reprogramme myself, by inserting a special silicone computer chip. [*eats potato chip. Emits computer noises. In robot monotone*] Decimal numbers and whole fractions loading into computer, decimal numbers and whole fractions loading into computer … [*normal voice*] And now I know where they are! A-ha! Found you, you creeps! It's okay, Dad, I'll save you— Whoops, thanks for the warning, Dad! I'm surrounded by evil scum!

[*He eats another chip, turns into death-dealing, invincible robot. Computer noises and gun battle*]

There. Got them all. We're safe now. It's okay, Dad. [*picks up father in his arms*] It's okay, don't cry. I know you're proud of me. 'Cause I'm as smart as your computers. And I'm proud of you, Dad, 'cause you're the one who programmed me.

VICTOR [*enters, sees* FARLEY, *checks his watch, writes*]
Twelve-oh-six and Farley's standing there holding his arms out—twelve-oh-six and five seconds and he sees me—

NIGHT LIGHT

FARLEY Victor!
VICTOR Whaat!
FARLEY [*approaching*] Victor, Victor good ol' Victor. How ya doin'?
VICTOR Twelve-oh-six and twenty seconds and I'm— good ol' Victor?
FARLEY Listen, Victor, I been thinking what you said about sitting next to me on the Math test.
VICTOR Look, I already told you, Farley, I'm not gonna—
FARLEY No no no. You were right.
VICTOR I was?
FARLEY We shouldn't cheat like that.
VICTOR We shouldn't?
FARLEY No, 'cause if we cheat like that, Miss Donaldson'll know. So let's cheat like this: you write out your Math notes on a crib sheet—
VICTOR Wait a minute—
FARLEY An' I'll hide it in my pocket an' look at it during the test, okay, ol' buddy?
VICTOR I can't do that.
FARLEY Whaddaya mean you can't do that?
VICTOR Twelve-oh-seven and thirteen seconds, asks what I mean I can't do that—
FARLEY I oughta smash your face in.
VICTOR Nineteen seconds, says he oughta smash my face in.
FARLEY What?
VICTOR Twenty-three seconds: says 'What?'
FARLEY Victor, you are gettin' weirder all the time.
VICTOR 'Weirder all the time,' thirty-one seconds.
FARLEY Victor, look!

[FARLEY *grabs* VICTOR's *lunchbag, runs*]

Stephen Aberle (VICTOR) and Brent Applegath (FARLEY)

VICTOR Thirty-five seconds: steals my lunch.
FARLEY This where ya keep your Math notes, Victor? In with your Pablum?
VICTOR [*getting smug*] Thirty-nine seconds, thinks I keep my Math notes with my Pablum.
FARLEY [*taking out a sandwich*] Baloney sandwich. Yuck.
VICTOR Forty-two seconds: baloney sandwich. Yuck.
FARLEY Howja like me to trash your lunch every day from now on?
VICTOR Forty-five seconds: scariest thing he can think of is squashing my lunch every—
FARLEY [*producing night light from bag*] Whoa. Hey! What's this here? A Snooky Bunny night light? Gee, most kids grow outa theirs when they're still babies.

But you still got yours, eh? Aaaawww. Widdle Victor scared of the dark.

[VICTOR *silently makes notes*]

Oh, you're not saying anything? So it's true? You're scared of the dark? Okay, Victor, have your little Snooky Bunny night light back. [FARLEY *tosses the night light to* VICTOR] Whatcha doin', writing a book or something?

[VICTOR *doesn't answer.* FARLEY *grabs him*]

Whatcha doing?
VICTOR It's an experiment.
FARLEY Oh. An experiment. How about if I do an experiment? [*grabs clipboard*] What if I experiment with keeping your clipboard?
VICTOR I need it!
FARLEY Too bad, eh.

[VICTOR *reaches for watch;* FARLEY *grabs* VICTOR'S *wrist*]

How many seconds now, Victor? Nice watch, Victor. Your sick father buy you that watch? Let's see. [*de-Velcros the watch from* VICTOR'S *wrist*]
VICTOR No! It's mine!

[FARLEY *runs to the jungle gym, climbs it.* VICTOR *chases him.* FARLEY *holds the watch over* VICTOR'S *head.* VICTOR *jumps for it*]

FARLEY Sixty-eight seconds! Victor jumps!

VICTOR [*overlapping*] Farley, gimme back my watch!
FARLEY One million seconds, Victor jumps higher! Ha ha haaa! [*runs off*]
VICTOR Far-leyyy! [*angrily stomps out of schoolyard and into bedroom*]

Bedroom

VICTOR *stomps in*

VICTOR All right, Tara, where's that book? I need that stupid book.
TARA [*entering*] I dunno where it is.
VICTOR [*starts cleaning up*] Look at this mess. No wonder you can't find anything in here. Did you put it in with your books? Your Pippi Longstockings?
TARA No, I didn't put it in with my books.
VICTOR No, of course not, you wouldn't put anything where it belongs, would you. Look at this.
TARA It isn't even my book. Why's it s'posed to be in my room?
VICTOR Because I left it here. Doggone it, Tara, the one time Mummy needs you to help out a little, and the one thing she needs you to do is clean up your room, and you don't even do that. Put these pens away.

[**VICTOR** *gathers up felts and paper, is about to dump them into the dresser drawer*]

TARA Not in there!
VICTOR Why not?

TARA The Monster!
VICTOR Too bad. [*dumps the felts in the drawer*]
TARA Victor, I hate you.
VICTOR Here it is.
TARA [*sneering*] 'Here it is.'
VICTOR [*leafing through book*] Now where's that stupid Monkey business?
TARA Did it work, Victor?
VICTOR No. I messed it up, okay? I get scared of everything.
TARA What about the Monster?
VICTOR That's not real.
TARA It is too.
VICTOR Farley's real. I got so scared. I just wanted to pound his face in—just pound him right into the dirt.
TARA Victor, that's not scared. That's mad. Don't you even know?
VICTOR Well, I got mad too, but only 'cause I was scared. When Farley gets mad, he just gets mad. He got mad today 'cause I wouldn't cheat with him on the Math test. And he's so scared of flunking—
TARA You just said he wasn't scared of anything.
VICTOR Yeah. [*pause*] He is scared. He's scared of flunking. That's great. That's great, Tara, thanks! [*runs out*]
TARA [*calls after him*] Victor, you never tell me anything!

Schoolyard

VICTOR *enters, perches on jungle gym, waits for* **FARLEY**.
FARLEY *enters; they watch each other*

FARLEY Victor. So. What are you gonna give me today?

Let's see ... You already gave me your lunch, that was nyahh—you gave me your clipboard, that was really boring—you tried to give me your little Snooky Bunny night light, but I figured you really needed that, eh—but you know what I really liked? This watch. Boy, this watch is ex. I'm gonna keep that for a long, long time. So what else you got for me?

VICTOR How come you're always so scared, Farley?

FARLEY Scared? Who's scared?

VICTOR You're scared.

FARLEY Are you crazy? You're the one who's always running from me.

VICTOR Am I?

FARLEY Yeah. Well, I'm not the one who's a chicken.

VICTOR Sure you are. You're scared of Math. Scared you're gonna flunk. And you will, too, you're not gonna pass. So you're never gonna be as smart as your father. He's gonna think you're a dummy.

FARLEY [*running across towards* VICTOR] I'll kill you!

VICTOR Don't you touch me or else!

FARLEY [*stops*] Or else what!

VICTOR Or else your father finds out I did all your Math.

FARLEY You're gonna tell? Tattle-tale!

VICTOR I don't have to tell. I just have to stop helping you. Which is what I'm gonna do. And he'll figure it out for himself, when you flunk this test, an' when you start bringing home zeros instead of tens. He's a smart guy, right? He'll say, 'What's going on, Farley? How come you got perfect in Math and now you're getting zeroes? Who's been doing your Math, Farley?'

FARLEY I'll tell him you were.

VICTOR And then he'll kill you.

FARLEY Maybe I'll kill you first.
VICTOR No, you won't. 'Cause if you want to pass, you need my help.
FARLEY I don't need no help.
VICTOR It's up to you, Farley. [*exit*]
FARLEY Wait a minute! Wait a minute! [*runs off after him*]

Bedroom

TARA, *alone, cuddles Kosmo on her bed*

TARA [*to Kosmo*] Daddy sure looked weird, eh, Kosmo? In the hospital? Mummy said he'll prob'ly come home soon. But I don't think so. His eyes were sort of wet, an' his face was all skinny an' sort of grey coloured …

[*As she talks, she grows more frightened. As she grows more frightened, the* MONSTER *rises up out of the dresser*]

Ohh, no! Not you again!
MONSTER Grrr.
TARA [*runs behind bed*] Oh, no you don't!
MONSTER Grrrr.
TARA Victor an' I showed you. We drew you an' tore you up.
MONSTER Grrrr.
TARA [*frightened*] So don't you come back here trying to scare me. You can't scare me. [*grabs paper, emerges from behind bed*] I'll show you, I'll draw another picture of you an' tear it up again. I've got my paper. Now all I need is— Oh, no. My felts.

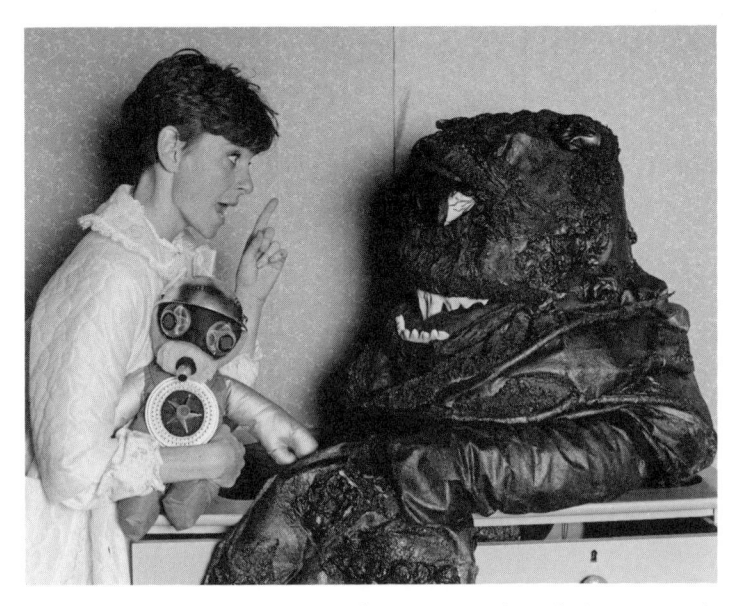

Carolyn Soper (TARA) and Brent Applegath (MONSTER)

MONSTER Huh?
TARA Victor put them in the dresser drawer with you.
MONSTER [*peers down into drawer, sees it is true, looks at* TARA] Nyah nyah nyah-nyah nyah!
TARA Look. I need them. You gotta let me have 'em. They're mine.
MONSTER [*emphatically, as in 'no way'*] Uh-uh.
TARA Will you lemme get them—if—if I draw a picture of you—an' I don't tear it up?
MONSTER Huh?
TARA I'll make it a real nice picture. An' then I won't tear it up. I promise. I'll do something nice with it. I know, I'll make it into a get-well card for my Daddy. 'Cause he's in hospital.
MONSTER [*surprised and sorry*] Ohhh.

TARA And everybody in the whole wide hospital, they'll all see this beautiful picture of you.
MONSTER [*pleased*] Oooh.
TARA You like that? Say 'Good.'
MONSTER Gooh.
TARA [*completing the word*] 'Duh.'
MONSTER Gooh. Duh.
TARA So I have to reach in there to get my felts. But you're not gonna bite me, are you?
MONSTER Gooh-d.
TARA No! Biting is bad.
MONSTER Bah-d?
TARA Yeah. Bad. 'Cause if you bite me, then I'm gonna open up like Daddy in the hospital and all my insides are gonna leak out. So you're not gonna bite me, are you?
MONSTER Naaawww.
TARA No?
MONSTER Nohh.
TARA Well. Okay. Here goes ... Okay.

[TARA *tentatively reaches in, takes out the felts.* MONSTER *watches.* TARA *yanks the felts out, startling both of them*]

Thank you.
MONSTER 'Ankyou.
TARA [*climbing onto bed—she takes out felts and begins drawing through this*] No, you say 'You're welcome.'
MONSTER 'Ur 'ell kuh.
VICTOR [*off*] Hey, Tara! Guess what!
TARA Hey, Victor, guess what. I'm teaching the Monster to talk.

VICTOR [*entering*] Tara—
TARA I'm teaching it to say 'Thank you, good, bad'—
MONSTER Y'r el-ka!
TARA Yeah, an' 'You're welcome.'
VICTOR Tara, Mummy just phoned.
TARA What?
VICTOR Daddy's temperature's down and he's fine. He comes home tomorrow.
TARA [*bouncing on bed*] Yaaayyy!
MONSTER Yaaayyy!
VICTOR [*looking around*] What was that?
TARA What?
VICTOR Weird, it sounded like an echo. Anyway, look what else. Rocky fixed your night light—and look what he did: he glued a little KosmoRoboTron on it.
TARA Oh, neat. Hey, look, Kosmo, just like you. [*puts it aside on the bed and resumes drawing*]
VICTOR Aren't you gonna try it out? Tara, do you know what I went through to get this for you? What about the Monster?
TARA Oh, we made friends.
VICTOR What? You made friends? I thought you hated each other.
TARA I don't hate it any more. I'm teaching it to talk, that's all.
VICTOR You're teaching it— Oh, no, that's right, I'm late. I gotta get going. [*runs out*]
TARA Hey Monster, you want a night light?
MONSTER Yeahhh.
TARA [*feeds night light to* MONSTER] Here. What do we say?
MONSTER 'Ank you.

TARA You're welcome.

[MONSTER *belches*]

TARA You say 'Excuse me.'
MONSTER 'Scuse 'ee.
TARA That's a good Monster. [*kisses it on the top of its head, exits*]
MONSTER Aaawww ... [*returns to dresser*]

Schoolyard

Enter VICTOR *and* FARLEY, *with Math books. Both are running out of patience*

VICTOR All right, lemme put it another way. The number after the decimal point tells you how many tenths. So point five is fiiive—what?
FARLEY I dunno.
VICTOR [*deep breath*] If the number after the decimal point shows how many tenths, then does point five mean five apples? Or five bunny rabbits? Or—
FARLEY Knock it off, five tenths.
VICTOR Very good.
FARLEY Watch it.
VICTOR You know this stuff, Farley, you're just afraid to admit it.
FARLEY Stop tellin' me what I know and teach me it.
VICTOR All right. So point five is—
FARLEY Five tenths.
VICTOR And five tenths is one what?

FARLEY One point five.
VICTOR No!
FARLEY [*grabs him*] Don't get mad at me! I can't do it when you get mad at me!
VICTOR Let go or I stop helping.
FARLEY [*lets go*] Just don't get mad at me, Victor. This is really hard, an' my head hurts, an' my father's gonna kill me, an' there's only three days left till the test.
VICTOR No, look, you're gonna do fine—
TARA [*runs on, carrying Kosmo*] Victor Victor Victor Victor Victor!
VICTOR Tara, please, we're trying to do some work here.
TARA But guess what? Daddy's home!
VICTOR Really?
TARA He's back just in time to get my get-well card.
VICTOR [*jumps up*] Great. [*to* FARLEY] I gotta go.
FARLEY Wait—what about tomorrow?
VICTOR Okay.
FARLEY An' you'll do my homework tonight?
VICTOR No. I told you. No more.
FARLEY Well, if I get mixed up can I call you?
VICTOR Yeah.
FARLEY Okay. [*as* VICTOR *starts to leave*] Uh—hey—
VICTOR What?
FARLEY Thanks.

[*Beat*]

VICTOR Okay.
TARA [*exiting with* VICTOR] Daddy said my Monster get-well card was scarier than the operation.

NIGHT LIGHT

VICTOR Told ya.

FARLEY [*left alone*] All right, what is this stupid thing here. Point five, uh—bunny rabbits—is the same way as saying—five tenths of a bunny rabbit. Ooh, that's gross. But five tenths—is the same thing as—one—half. Hey! Victor, I got it! I got it! Point five equals a half a bunny rabbit! [*runs off after them*]

SECRETS

Production History

Secrets was first performed by Green Thumb Theatre at David Thompson High School, Vancouver, on February 20, 1992, with the following cast:

BINNIE / BROOKE, Ruth McIntosh
SUSAN / HEATHER, Laura Myers
VICTOR / GREG, Bruce Harwood
ROCKY / CALVIN, Chris McGregor

Director: Patrick MacDonald
Assistant Director: Robert Metcalfe
Set and Costume Designer: Ted Roberts
Mask Design and Construction: Val Arntzen
Stage Manager: Angela Beaulieu

Subsequently it was produced by Magnus Theatre Lab (Thunder Bay) and Young People's Theatre (Toronto).

Acknowledgements

My thanks to Green Thumb for commissioning this, and to Patrick MacDonald, Robert Metcalfe, Emma Lazarus, and Jill Weiss of the P.I.D. Society for notes and advice.

Characters

There are four actors. They play four bare-faced principals, and four masked characters.

VICTOR doubles as GREG
SUSAN doubles as HEATHER
BINNIE doubles as BROOKE
ROCKY doubles as CALVIN

All characters are in their mid-teens. The actors wear neutral clothes, distinguished by accessories, jackets, etc. to facilitate quick changes. The Principals are non-conformists; the Masks' accessories are more fashionable.

Setting and Structure

This is a one-act play, without intermission, but it is divided into two so-called 'Acts.' 'Act I' takes place during the day, in and around a high school. The settings may suggest a classroom, cafeteria, corridor, etc. 'Act II' takes place at a party at night, in two areas of VICTOR's house: the front porch, and the bedroom of the absent Tara, VICTOR's little sister from *Night Light*.

Taped sound of student noise throughout, for populating the school, the street and the party. Rock music at the party.

ACT I

The bell goes. Taped sound of between-classes chaos. Enter GREG *and* CALVIN *in one area,* HEATHER *and* BROOKE *in another. A semi-coherent, comic impression of noise, energy and confusion*

BROOKE Oh, nobody dresses like that any more in L.A.
HEATHER Really?
GREG Oh, she's an animal.
CALVIN Susan? Oh, yeah.
BROOKE Oh, yeah, coming here is like taking a time warp back two years.
GREG She's been with a lotta guys.
CALVIN Oh, I know.
HEATHER Oh, I know.
CALVIN She told me herself.
HEATHER People here go down to L.A. to find out what people are actually wearing.
GREG She's had her fair share.
BROOKE It's sort of nice up here, though.
CALVIN Hey, tell me about it.
BROOKE I mean it's sort of charming and old-fashioned. Once you get used to the slow pace.
CALVIN She's tough, though. You gotta know what you're getting into, if you catch my, like, drift.
HEATHER We have some big names from here too, you know. Rock stars, movie stars—

SECRETS

Ruth McIntosh (BROOKE), Chris McGregor (CALVIN), Bruce Harwood (GREG) and Laura Myers (HEATHER)

GREG Actually I think she's a bit crazy, if you want to know the truth.
BROOKE I'm sure you do.
HEATHER [*crossing to* GREG] Gre-eg! Yo!
GREG Hey, Babe. [*to* CALVIN] Not a word.
CALVIN You neither.
HEATHER So did I just overhear you talking about Susan?

[*Brief silence, for the first time*]

GREG Uh—yeah, just, you know.
HEATHER Yeah, well, that's what I thought. Gee, I wonder why. [*exit*]
GREG What's that supposed to mean? She expects me to run after her an' beg for her forgiveness?
CALVIN When hell freezes over, right?

GREG Did you tell her something?
CALVIN No! You told everybody. [*giggles, to* BROOKE] Typical. Soap opera around here. Welcome to Canada, eh?
BROOKE How exciting for you all. Eh.

[*Enter* SUSAN]

GREG Hey, Susan.
SUSAN What?
GREG Nothin'. Just—hey.
BROOKE Hello. I caught your little performance in Lit today. Yelling at the teacher about Shakespeare. Very dramatic, I thought. Especially when she threw you out.
SUSAN Like I asked.
CALVIN Whoops! Whoa!
GREG [*close to her*] You going to this party tonight at Victor's?
SUSAN No.
GREG You stayin' home tonight? You wanna come on out with me later? Know what I mean?
SUSAN You know what I'd really like to do tonight? Come here, I'll whisper.
GREG Oh, yeah?

[*He leans in. She whispers in his ear. He pulls away*]

Aw, man—that is the most *obscene*—that is the *grossest*—
CALVIN What'd she say?
GREG That is *so sexist*, Susan, that is just—
SUSAN Get outa here.

SECRETS

CALVIN What'd she say! What'd she say!
GREG You want me to repeat that? I'm tryin' to stop thinkin' about it!

[*The two boys exit*]

SUSAN [*to* BROOKE] Sometimes you gotta shock them a little, right? Just to stop them drooling on you.
BROOKE Really? I've heard you like nothing better than a little male drool. Bye. [*exit*]
SUSAN [*to audience*] Boy, does she belong with that bunch. Been here one week and she's right in with the in crowd. They all think they're so cool. What a cow.
  Course, that's what she thinks of me too. Not the cool part, of course. Just the cow part. That's my reputation around here. Miss Sex and Violence [*year of performance*]. Supposedly. They have no idea how scared I am. Nobody knows. That's fine with me. It's my secret.
  Instead, they think I'm this regular nympho. 'Oh, yeah, Susan. Susan's hot stuff, Susan's easy,' blah blah blah.
BINNIE [*off*] Susan!
SUSAN Yo, Binnie!
BINNIE [*enters, carrying two bags, hers and* ROCKY*'s*] Hey, how ya doin'?
SUSAN Same old same old.
BINNIE [*sits*] Gee, that's funny, me too. [*takes out make-up and/or hairbrush. Offers make-up*] Want some?
SUSAN No thanks, I'm trying to cut down.
BINNIE [*grooming biz*] So I heard you got kicked out of English Lit today.
SUSAN Yeah, I expressed an opinion.

BINNIE Oh, Susan, gotta stop doin' that. This is school.
SUSAN I know. Bad habit. [*observes* BINNIE*'s bags*] Jeez, you're looking like a keener today. Two book bags.
BINNIE Oh, yeah. This one's Rocky's. He left it at my place last night.
SUSAN [*aside*] Rocky's Binnie's boyfriend. Her mother found out they're making love, and she freaked out. [*in*] Your mother let him in the house?
BINNIE Well, we kind of sorted that out. I told her we're engaged to be married, an' faithful to each other, an' into safe sex. Finally I said she might as well get used to it, 'cause I'm never gonna be a virgin again.
SUSAN That's not bad.
BINNIE Yeah, she cried for a while an' then she calmed down. So he was over last night, and he's coming to pick me up tonight and stuff. You are going to this party at Victor's?
SUSAN No.
BINNIE No? Everybody's going. I thought one of the guys invited you.
SUSAN Three of the guys invited me. All for the same reason. So I said no.
BINNIE Was one of them Victor?
SUSAN No. Why? [*aside*] Victor's this slightly weird intellectual kind of guy who doesn't fit in any of the regular groups. A little like me. He's nice—fairly cute in his own way—but everybody's saying he's— [*in*] Haven't you heard this rumour going around about Victor?
BINNIE You mean this thing that he's supposed to be gay?
SUSAN Yeah.
BINNIE Yeah, I heard that. It's not true.

SECRETS

SUSAN [*aside*] Sure she's gonna say that, she and Rocky are Victor's best friends. [*in*] Well, he didn't ask me.

BINNIE And you don't want to go alone?

SUSAN When I go alone, they say things behind my back, and they all hit on me and grab me and stuff.

BINNIE Susan, that is grim.

SUSAN No, really? [*re* ROCKY*'s bag*] Hey, y'ever wonder what Rocky carries around in there?

BINNIE Why—textbooks and homework.

BINNIE & SUSAN [*together*] Not!

BINNIE Actually it's prob'ly all car parts an' porno mags.

SUSAN No doubt.

BINNIE No, wait, let's be fair, he does have a couple of books. 'Cause Victor's helping him on Math.

SUSAN Come on, Bin. I dare ya.

BINNIE Forget it! Rocky an' I made a solemn pact. We swore we'd respect each other's privacy.

SUSAN Oh, really? Oh, really? Like the night we found him outside your window?

BINNIE That was a joke.

SUSAN So's this.

BINNIE He was just doing that to be obnoxious.

SUSAN So are we.

BINNIE [*pause*] All right.

SUSAN All right!

[*They dig through* ROCKY*'s bag. They take out some small car parts, a couple of textbooks and a* Penthouse]

BINNIE What'd I tell you.

SUSAN You know your man, I'll give you that. Whoa! You still writing him love notes after all these years?

[SUSAN *takes out a sheet of paper with computer-graphics hearts and flowers, and typing*]

BINNIE No. 'Dear Rocky.'
SUSAN 'Thank you for an unforgettable evening.'
BINNIE 'Let it—'
SUSAN 'Be our little secret. Hugs and kisses—and wild animal cries— Your Secret Squeeze.' [*silence. Aside*] Oh, man …
BINNIE Well, it's a joke.
SUSAN Well, of course it is.
BINNIE Prob'ly from one of the guys in Computer Science. Prob'ly Victor. Doing one of his little pretend jokes. [*aside*] I hope.
SUSAN Well, sure. Look, everything's spelled right, it must be Victor. [*aside*] Maybe.
BINNIE Well! Better put this back. [*stuffs everything back into bag*]
SUSAN You gonna ask him about it?
BINNIE Are you kidding? How can I ask without telling him we were snooping?
SUSAN [*aside*] Oh, God, she really does suspect something.
BINNIE And I mean, anyway, there's nothing to ask. It's a joke, that's all. 'Cause everybody knows me and Rocky have total commitment.
SUSAN Well, right, of course. [*aside*] Except you keep hearing things … [*in*] Listen, I'm late, I gotta go. But, you know, if you want to talk or whatever.
BINNIE What about? [*beat*] Okay. Thanks. I'll see ya tonight at the party, okay? Are you coming, or what?
SUSAN I dunno.

SECRETS

BINNIE Come with me an' Rocky. We'll protect you from the heavy hitters.
SUSAN Well, we'll see. Take it easy, Bin.

[*Exit* SUSAN. BINNIE *may get up and cross to the cafeteria for a change of scene. If so, cafeteria sound*]

BINNIE [*to audience*] That's what I get for looking for stuff. I find stuff.
CALVIN [*enters*] Hey, you seen Rocky around?
BINNIE He's in shop.
CALVIN Listen, tell him Greg and me want him to look at our truck, okay, it's running weird.
BINNIE 'Kay.
CALVIN Maybe tonight, at this dumb party at Victor's. You going?
BINNIE I dunno. You?
CALVIN Yeah. He's a jackass, of course, but he's got a big house, an' there hasn't been a party for a while. So if it's boring, we'll all leave. I'm takin' that hot babe from L.A.
BINNIE Good for you.
CALVIN We're goin' with Greg an' Heather. We're celebrating. Heather got an A in Computer Science.
BINNIE No kidding. Heather takes Computer Science? Isn't that interesting.
CALVIN [*passes* VICTOR *entering*] Yo, Victor! Party tonight!
VICTOR [*uncertain what the word means*] Yo. [*enters. Sits and unpacks his lunch*] Binnerama! Binmeister! The Binster doing lunch!
BINNIE Victor, Victor, Boa Constrictor! Y'all ready for tonight?

JOHN LAZARUS

VICTOR Hey. Gonna party hearty. Gonna party down an' party back up again.
BINNIE I hear everybody's going.
VICTOR Yeah, it seems to have got out of hand.
BINNIE Everybody except Susan.
VICTOR [*alarmed*] What? Why not?
BINNIE 'Cause she doesn't want to go alone. An' all the guys who invited her are sleazebags. None of the non-sleazebags invited her, Victor. Not even you, Victor.
VICTOR [*aside*] How did she know about my thing for Susan?
BINNIE Invite her, Victor.
VICTOR She's invited. Everybody's invited.
BINNIE I mean invite her special. As your date.
VICTOR Don't be silly. I couldn't. I mean, why bother.
BINNIE She wants you to, Victor.
VICTOR She does? [*aside*] Wow.
BINNIE She does. [*aside*] Maybe. Course she also thinks he's a homo, but I think I'll spare him that part of it ...
VICTOR I'll think about it.
BINNIE Whatsamatter? Scared?
VICTOR [*aside*] How does she know? [*in*] Don't be absurd. Of course I'm not scared. Maybe I'm just not that interested.
BINNIE In Susan? You? Not interested? C'mon, Victor.
VICTOR [*aside*] She always sees right through me. I hate that. [*in*] Well, maybe I'll invite her just to shut you up.
BINNIE Atta boy. That's what we like to hear. Go get her. No pain, no gain. [*gets up to leave*] Hey, listen. Did you write, uh—
VICTOR What?
BINNIE Oh, nothing, never mind. [*aside*] Can't ask him

SECRETS

about the note without him knowing I looked. And if he knows, Rocky'll know. [*in*] Catch you later, Studley. [*exit*]

VICTOR 'Studley.' Gimme a break. [*to audience*] Wow. Susan wants me to ask her out? Unless Binnie's just trying to get me to make an ass of myself.

'Susan, would you care to attend this little soirée as my evening companion? Nothing special, no pressure, very low-key—a few friends, some fine wine, a little Beethoven, a little LSD, some sexual intercourse, maybe get married,' oh, help! How do all those jerks do it!

[ROCKY *enters behind him, carrying a chain and looking like a dangerous juvenile offender*]

You always have to act like you know exactly how to do everything. Anything that's for the first time, you can never let on it's the first time, you know? How do the rest of them manage? Everybody knows how except the genius!

ROCKY Now let's see. What am I gonna do to Victor today?

[VICTOR *hears this, sits still*]

I think maybe I'll tie one end of this chain 'round his ankles and the other end to my car, and drag him 'round the school a few times. [*comes forward to* VICTOR] So you gonna come quiet, or do I gotta beat the daylights outa ya first?

[*Pause*]

Bruce Harwood (VICTOR) and Chris McGregor (ROCKY)

VICTOR [*face to face*] You never just take me out to dinner any more.

[ROCKY *tries to keep a straight face, but can't.* VICTOR *cracks up.* ROCKY *shoves* VICTOR]

ROCKY [*shoves him*] Flake off, jerk!
VICTOR [*shoves back*] Jerk off, flake! [*laughs some more. Aside*] I kill myself.
ROCKY Yeah, yeah, yeah ... [*sits beside* VICTOR] Hey, listen, man, it's one thing to joke around like that when we're hangin' out down the garage. But when you flip your wrists an' stuff at the guys around here, they don't know you're kidding.

SECRETS

VICTOR Oh, come on!

ROCKY I'm tellin' you, you keep that stuff goin', it's gonna come back an' get you. [*opens his lunch*]

[*They eat*]

VICTOR So where's your books?

ROCKY What?

VICTOR We were supposed to work on the Math, remember?

ROCKY Oh, yeah. I left all my stuff at Binnie's last night. [*aside*] With a note inside it from Whatsername. If she looks, I'm in deep sludge.

VICTOR Oh, for Pete's sake. You just missed her. I saw she had your bag, but it didn't register.

ROCKY Oh, yeah? Where? [*calls*] Binnie!

VICTOR No, she's gone.

ROCKY Well, I phoned her this morning an' she said she'd bring it to class.

VICTOR Hey man, the whole point was to have it *before* class. *Now.* At *lunch* hour. I was gonna save your hide, remember?

ROCKY Yeah, I know, sorry.

VICTOR Rocky, I can't help you with this crap if you're not even gonna bring your books. I'm not your mother, okay?

ROCKY Then stop talkin' like her, okay?

VICTOR Well, I mean, really.

ROCKY Do I talk to you like that when I'm givin' you the driving lessons?

VICTOR No, you scream obscenities at me.

ROCKY Exactly. [*sees* HEATHER *and* BROOKE *approaching, off. Aside*] Oh, Jeez. Trouble on the hoof.

HEATHER [*enters with* BROOKE, *passing through*] Hello, Rocky.
ROCKY Yeah.
HEATHER Victor.
VICTOR Darling.
ROCKY Stop that!
VICTOR Chill.
BROOKE What's the big chain for?
ROCKY Body work.
BROOKE Oh?
ROCKY *Cars.* Straightenin' out *bent cars.*
VICTOR [*aside*] See? Nobody ever flirts with me like that.
HEATHER You coming to the party tonight?
ROCKY Yeah. With Binnie.
HEATHER Oh, good. So are we. See you there. [*as they exit*] Victor, darling, it's going to be the event of the season!
VICTOR I know, darling, I'm simply moist with anticipation.
ROCKY Hey! Stop it! Jeez, I hate when you do that.
VICTOR Hey. It's a joke, Jackass.
ROCKY Hey. I know it's a joke, Dipstick. Jus' don' do it when I'm sittin' next to ya!
VICTOR Take it easy. You're so sensitive.
ROCKY *Stop it!*
VICTOR I wasn't doing it that time! That was me!
ROCKY Oh.

[*They eat in silence*]

[*aside*] Well, the guy's got a right to know. He's gonna find out anyways. [*in*] Look, just knock off jokin' like that, okay? 'Cause ya know what Greg's sayin'?

SECRETS

VICTOR No, and who cares.
ROCKY He's tellin' everybody he's wearin' surgical gloves to your party, 'cause he doesn't wanna get AIDS.
VICTOR What? From who?
ROCKY From you. Him an' Calvin an' them are goin' around seriously sayin' you're gay. An' people believe 'em.
VICTOR What? Come on. Nobody believes those guys. Do they?

[*No answer*]

Really? Are you serious?
ROCKY It's kind of getting around the school, man.
VICTOR It is? Why didn't you tell me this?
ROCKY I am. I been tryin' to.
VICTOR But—but it's a running gag, it's like somebody doing imitations of, uh—
ROCKY Not the way they're sayin' it.
VICTOR Really? This is, like, widespread? Girls too?
ROCKY You just saw.
VICTOR But it's a joke! Everybody does it! You do those jokes so they'll know you're *not* one! How come when *I* do it, it means I *am*?
ROCKY Maybe you're more convincing.
VICTOR Oh, thanks a lot!
ROCKY Sorry. All right, maybe also 'cause of that letter you wrote to the school paper. About how it's okay to be gay.
VICTOR That was because of that guy in Grade Eleven who got the spit kicked out of him. All I said was they shouldn't beat him up.
ROCKY Well, so it means you're big on gay rights.

VICTOR Yeah, but not for *me*, I'm *straight!* Oh, my God, I bet you're right. How stupid of me, eh. How dare I suggest people should live and let live.

ROCKY Well, I stood up for ya, man. I told them guys you're my friend and you're one hundred percent hetero.

VICTOR Really? You said that?

ROCKY I did. I told 'em you been workin' at the garage, an' that you shoot a good game of golf, you know, all the guy stuff.

VICTOR Well, thank you, my man.

[*Esoteric handshake*]

ROCKY Hey. I'll stick by you.

VICTOR A true friend.

ROCKY Just till they start sayin' I'm one too, an' then I'm outa here.

VICTOR Oh, great, thanks a lot.

ROCKY No sweat, man.

VICTOR Rocky, how am I supposed to fight something like this?

ROCKY I know. It's rough. But just think how you'd feel if you were one. So you couldn't even say you weren't.

VICTOR If I *were* one, I wouldn't mind them saying so!

ROCKY You wouldn't? You sure? Like that poor jerk they beat up? How do you think he feels?

VICTOR Yeah, I guess you're right.

ROCKY [*aside*] I dunno if I should tell him the other thing. Might just make it worse. Except he oughta know what he's up against here. [*in*] All right, Victor, the other thing those guys are saying is, any guy who

hasn't done it by the time he's seventeen must be one.
VICTOR What? Why does that mean I'm gay?
ROCKY I know, it's—
VICTOR I mean, even if I'd never done it, why would that— Who says I haven't done it? I've done it dozens of times!
ROCKY Well, hey, I know that. [*aside*] Not. [*in*] Look, Victor, those guys got untreated sewage for brains, everybody knows that.
VICTOR Why do they think I've never done it?
ROCKY 'Cause nobody knows anybody you've done it with.
VICTOR They were all during summer vacations.
ROCKY Look, Victor, there's nothing wrong with waiting for the right woman, you know?
VICTOR I am not waiting! I've done it! Lots!
ROCKY Okay, I'm just sayin'. A guy doesn't have to have sex to be cool—
VICTOR What is this, Socials Nine?
ROCKY I'm only sayin', there's lotsa guys around who've never had it, and they're still great guys. You'd be surprised.
VICTOR Easy for you to say, Wilt the Stilt.
ROCKY Hey. What Binnie and I have is special.
VICTOR All right. Sorry.
ROCKY [*aside*] What a liar. He's right. I got no right to preach at him.

[ROCKY *resumes eating,* VICTOR *frets.* BINNIE *enters, unseen behind them*]

VICTOR [*to audience*] This is a disaster. This is two disasters. I don't know which is worse, that they're saying

I'm a homosexual or saying I'm a virgin. I need a girlfriend. Actually, what I need is for everybody to know I have a girlfriend. Well, I also need a girlfriend, but that's a third disaster entirely.
  [*checks his watch. In*] Twelve fifty-one and seventeen seconds, gotta go, Rocky. I'm a man with a mission. I'm inviting Susan to the party.
ROCKY Hey, go for it, man.

[*Esoteric handshake*]

VICTOR Thanks. [*stands, sees* BINNIE *behind them*] Aaghh!
BINNIE Susan, eh? About time.
VICTOR Binnie, this is absolutely top secret. For now. You tell anybody and you are dead meat.
ROCKY Hey.
BINNIE 'Dead meat'?
VICTOR Sorry.
BINNIE Don't you threaten me, ya knob. That is so insulting!
VICTOR Okay, sorry.
BINNIE I'm on your side! I been wanting to see you an' her get together for years, ya clam brain.
VICTOR Really? Oh.
BINNIE I will keep your precious little secret.
VICTOR Okay. Thanks. But later on, if this turns into something, then I'm gonna want you to tell everybody on earth.
BINNIE Hey. My specialty. Break a leg. [*kisses his cheek*]
VICTOR Thank you, I think. [*to* ROCKY] Au revoir, dude.
ROCKY Yeah.

SECRETS

[VICTOR *exits*]

BINNIE So hi.
ROCKY So hi.

[*They kiss*]

BINNIE [*aside, if there is an audience reaction*] Oh, grow up. [*in*] So how ya doin'?
ROCKY I'm good. So how are you?
BINNIE Great. Perfect. Here's your stuff. [*gives him the bag*]
ROCKY [*looking at her carefully*] Yeah, thanks. [*aside*] She seems okay. [*in*] Find anything interesting in there?
BINNIE [*aside*] He can tell I looked. [*in*] I didn't look, dummy. [*aside*] It's all over my face.
ROCKY [*aside*] Yeah, maybe.
BINNIE [*aside*] I'm a liar. I am a rotten human being.
ROCKY [*aside*] I got it! Head her off at the pass! [*in*] Listen, I gotta show you something, this is hysterical. Check this out. [*digs in bag*]
BINNIE [*aside*] Oh, no—he's not gonna—oh, Rocky.
ROCKY [*produces note*] Get this. From one of the guys in Computer Science. [*shows it to her*] 'Wild animal cries.' Isn't that a hoot?
BINNIE [*reads it*] Hot stuff. Who did this?
ROCKY I dunno. Somebody snuck it into my bag. Prob'ly Victor. [*aside*] Victor'll say no, but that's okay.
BINNIE You sure it wasn't a girl?
ROCKY [*shrugs*] Maybe. Everybody does stuff like that on the computers. Who knows.
BINNIE [*aside*] I am so stupid! When am I gonna learn to trust him! [*she hugs him*]

170

ROCKY Whoa, baby. [*aside*] Amazing what you can come up with when your life depends on it.

[*Enter* SUSAN, *in another area.* VICTOR *intercepts her*]

VICTOR Hey! Susan! How ya doin'.
SUSAN Okay.
VICTOR [*nodding*] Cool.
SUSAN [*aside*] Oh, please.
VICTOR [*aside*] Oh, help. [*in*] Uh, were you figuring on coming to my party tonight?
SUSAN No.
VICTOR Oh. [*aside*] Well, that broke the ice. Okay, here goes. [*in*] Well, I was wondering if you would like to, uh— Whether you would care to, uh—
SUSAN [*aside*] I hate this stuff.
VICTOR How would you feel about attending this little soirée as my personal date? [*aside, wincing*] 'Soirée'!
SUSAN Why?
VICTOR 'Why'? [*aside*] What does she mean, 'Why'? [*in*] What do you mean, 'Why'? For—you know, for fun. For the pleasure of each other's company. [*aside*] Because I'm madly in love with you. [*in*] Just for the heck of it, how's that?
SUSAN Good reason.
VICTOR So? What do you say?
SUSAN [*aside*] If it's true he's gay, then why is he— Oh, of course. [*in*] First I want you to tell me your real reason.
VICTOR What? What do you mean? [*aside*] Does everybody know how I feel?
SUSAN Well—Victor—look, you're inviting me because of this rumour that you're gay, aren't you?

SECRETS

VICTOR [*aside*] Gets right to the point, doesn't she. [*in*] No! I'm inviting you because I really—uh—
SUSAN You want to kind of make a statement.
VICTOR Yeah. But also—I mean, if I gotta invite some girl, it might as well be you. [*aside*] Well, that swept her off her feet. End of dream. [*in*] Well, thanks for considering it, anyway.
SUSAN Just a minute. I didn't say no.
VICTOR You mean you're saying yes?
SUSAN I'm thinking.
VICTOR Oh.

[*She thinks,* **VICTOR** *waits. Meanwhile, back at* **ROCKY** *and* **BINNIE**]

BINNIE [*aside, in hug*] I gotta tell him. [*in*] Rocky, I gotta tell you something. I been such a dork.
ROCKY Hey, don't you talk like that about my girl.
BINNIE I broke our agreement, Rocky. I looked in your bag.
ROCKY [*aside*] Wow! I called it right! [*in*] You looked in my bag?
BINNIE Yeah. Susan an' I were— [*aside*] No, leave her out of it, it's my own fault. [*in*] I got no excuse. I just looked, that's all.
ROCKY Oh, Jeez, Binnie, you must think I'm such a pig.
BINNIE Well, I wasn't sure what—
ROCKY You found the magazine, right?
BINNIE Oh! No, I wasn't even thinking of that!
ROCKY Sorry.
BINNIE You're sorry? What're you sorry for? *I* snooped in your bag, *I* found the note—an' I thought something was going on.

ROCKY What do you mean?
BINNIE The note. I thought it was for real.

[ROCKY *stares at her for a minute, then laughs out loud and hugs her*]

ROCKY Oh, baby, you are something.
BINNIE Oh, Rocky …
ROCKY Hey. Hey, silly, don't cry.
BINNIE I'm not. I'm relieved. I just need for you to forgive me.
ROCKY Well, sure I forgive you.
BINNIE Okay. I love you so much.
ROCKY Me too. I love you too. [*aside, in embrace*] I am a louse. I am gonna rot in hell.
BINNIE Listen, I gotta go. You're picking me up tonight, remember?
ROCKY You think I'd forget?
BINNIE I'm sorry. I'm sorry. I don't deserve you.
ROCKY Stop it!
BINNIE Love ya! [*kisses him, exits, laughing*] I am such an idiot!
ROCKY [*to audience*] She's right. She doesn't deserve me. She deserves a human being.

[*Back to* VICTOR *and* SUSAN]

VICTOR [*aside*] Still thinking. What's she got to think about? Why doesn't she just laugh in my face, kick me in the testicles and get it over with?
SUSAN [*aside*] See, if I go as his date, they'll all make jokes. But also, they won't be leaning on me all night.

SECRETS

And Victor seems pretty safe.

VICTOR [*aside*] Everybody says she jumps into bed with a guy if he buys her a drink. I don't believe that, but— Me, she has to go into heavy meditation before she'll decide to spend an evening standing *next* to.

SUSAN [*aside*] And wouldn't it be nice to have a date with a guy who isn't grabbing and groping and expecting me to— [*in*] Victor, I'd love to be your date this evening. Thank you for asking me.

VICTOR What? Wow. Great. That's great. I—that's just—that's just great. Oh, *thank* you.

SUSAN Okay.

VICTOR No, I mean it, you don't know— *Thank* you.

SUSAN Victor, we don't have to pretend this date is something it isn't.

VICTOR No. [*aside*] What?

SUSAN I mean, I know it's just to shut them all up.

VICTOR Well, it isn't entirely—

SUSAN I can understand if you've had enough of that stuff. I do think what you've already done was very brave.

VICTOR Thank you! [*aside*] She thinks I'm brave! What the heck is she talking about? [*in*] What was brave?

SUSAN Well, that letter to the school paper defending that boy in Grade Eleven, you know, the, uh—

VICTOR The homosexual.

SUSAN Yeah. Which made it pretty obvious, you know, that, uh—

VICTOR That I'm—that I'm—

SUSAN Well, yeah.

VICTOR Gay.

SUSAN Yeah.

VICTOR I'm not.
SUSAN You're not?
VICTOR No. Never have been. Never will be. I promise.
SUSAN Oh! Well. Okay. There you go.
VICTOR You thought I was?
SUSAN Well, uh—
VICTOR Susan, I wrote the letter because I happen to not think it's a crime if somebody's gay. Somebody else. It doesn't mean I'm one!
SUSAN Oh, well, that's nice.
VICTOR Listen. There's obviously been a little misunderstanding here. If you want to change your mind—
SUSAN No! No. I said I'd go out with you tonight, and I will.
VICTOR [*aside*] Oh, great, she's dating me 'cause she has to. Perfect. [*in*] Well, I—appreciate that, Susan. Thank you.
SUSAN My pleasure.
VICTOR [*aside*] How do you get back to small talk from here?
SUSAN [*aside*] This is getting highly strained. I'm outa here. [*in*] Well. See you tonight.
VICTOR Okay. Great. See you tonight.

[*She exits.* VICTOR *remains, in silence*]

ROCKY [*to audience*] Don't get me wrong, I do care about her. We been best friends since we were kids. So, you know, a couple of years ago we start going out, an' then we start having a little—you know—sex. And next thing you know, she acts like we're already married. And I don't want to be married! But I can't tell her that! So I lie.

SECRETS

VICTOR [*to audience*] She's going in my direction. But I can't go with her now, you know, it would seem kind of weird, so I have to wait here for a while so I won't be schlepping down the street a half a block behind her. 'Cause that wouldn't be cool.

ROCKY I started lying to her the first time I got involved with another girl. If you call a half an hour in the back of a truck 'involved.' But then once you start lying like that, you have to keep doing it, right? And then the lies keep getting bigger on you. But you're only lying so you won't hurt people. Including yourself.

VICTOR The hardest thing I've ever had to do in my whole life is to learn how to be cool.

ROCKY Cool. Everybody thinks I'm so cool. I am not cool. I pretend nothing bothers me, but inside I feel like everybody else has got it all figured out except me. I wish I was smart like Victor.

VICTOR I think being cool means pretending things aren't important when they are. Things like giving Susan time to walk home so I won't be trailing after her. Or like everybody being scared and lonely and screwed-up, and never able to tell each other how we really feel 'cause the other guy's just as scared and trying just as hard to be cool.

[*They exit, separately*]

ACT II

The setting is now VICTOR'*s house. Rock music and party noise. Enter* HEATHER *and* BROOKE. *They do the set change*

HEATHER What do you think? Isn't he prime?
BROOKE Rocky? Oh, he's fairly edible.
HEATHER He's great. Believe me.
BROOKE I'm sure. And here we are stuck with those two.
HEATHER Oh, those two aren't so bad. You get used to them.
BROOKE What a delightful thought. Where are they, anyway?
HEATHER They went to pick up some fuel.

[*Enter* GREG *and* CALVIN, *with beer and/or booze. Again, much overlap and noise*]

GREG Hey! Guess what we heard!
CALVIN Susan is coming as Victor's date!
HEATHER Really?
BROOKE You mean it's a costume party?
HEATHER You have got to be kidding.
CALVIN Isn't that hilarious?
BROOKE Odd couple of the year.
GREG Why would Victor invite a girl?
CALVIN 'Specially that one.

HEATHER Maybe all the guys turned him down.
BROOKE Maybe she *is* a guy. Maybe she's been a drag queen all along.
GREG Susan? I don't think so.
HEATHER Oh, and you'd know, wouldn't you?
GREG Maybe. Listen, I'm goin' back to the car an' have a smoke. [*to* CALVIN] Wanna?
CALVIN No, I wanna keep my wits about me tonight.
BROOKE Oh, don't bother on my account.
GREG Hey, at least with Victor she doesn't have to worry about gettin' molested. Not that she ever does, except when she's worried it won't happen, yuk yuk yuk. [*exit*]
BROOKE He only talks like that because he's insecure about his own sexuality.
HEATHER Oh, absolutely. I know that. He can be a total creep. [*to* CALVIN] Frankly, I don't know why you hang around with him.
CALVIN What? What're you talking about? You hang around with him too.
HEATHER That's different. I have to hang around with him. He's my boyfriend.
VICTOR [*enters onto porch*] Hi, guys.
CALVIN Victor! Yoo-hoo! Oh, you look simply divine in that outfit!
VICTOR Have you ever considered therapy?
CALVIN Oh, very funny, look who's talking, eh.
VICTOR I give up, your wit renders me speechless. Listen, there's drinks in the fridge, and there's, you know, food, and, um, have a good time.
HEATHER [*as the Masks exit into the house*] Thanks, Victor.
BROOKE Thank you, Victor. What an adorable house.

CALVIN I hear you're with Susan tonight. That's really nice.

[VICTOR *stops him*]

What? What? What'd I say?
VICTOR Take it easy.
CALVIN Hey. All I said, I thought it was nice. You and Susan. Really nice. You got a problem with that?
VICTOR No. Do you?
CALVIN I got no problem, Victor. I never have a problem. Swell party so far. [*exit*]
VICTOR [*to audience*] Swell. Just swell. I'm so scared I've forgotten how to sweat. What was I thinking of! This is the first party I've ever thrown. I tell a few friends, my family's away for the weekend, party at my place—but then the mainstream crowd catches on and it becomes this huge crossover hit. Prob'ly 'cause they think this is one of those parties that if your parents find out, they disown you. The secret is that I have my folks' permission to do this. But if these guys knew that, they'd trash the place.

So I'm going nuts worrying that the party's gonna be a success, and worrying about the house and everything. And so of course I choose tonight to invite the girl of my dreams on our first date! Recipe for apocalypse.
SUSAN [*coming up to the porch*] Hi.
VICTOR Oh! Hi!
SUSAN [*aside*] Hell begins.
VICTOR You look great! [*aside*] She looks great!
SUSAN Thank you. [*aside*] I look the same as always.
VICTOR My bedroom's the second door down.

SUSAN Hey, don't waste any time or anything.
VICTOR [*aside*] Blaarrgghh! [*in*] I meant, for your coat. Everybody's dumping their jackets and stuff on my bed, that's all I meant— Oh! Hi!
ROCKY [*enters with* BINNIE, *chanting*] Par-tee! Par-tee! Par-tee! Par-tee! ...

[ROCKY *does his esoteric handshake with* VICTOR]

BINNIE Will you cut that out? What a dork.
VICTOR No, listen, that's what this party needs. Hi. [*kisses* BINNIE]
SUSAN Hi, guys.
BINNIE [*looking the couple over appraisingly*] Well! Nice to see you two.
VICTOR All right. Listen, jackets and coats go in my bedroom and there's drinks in the kitchen. [*to* SUSAN] Would you like me to get you a drink?
SUSAN You got, like, a ginger ale or something?
VICTOR Sure. Right this way. You guys coming?
BINNIE In a second. You go ahead.

[VICTOR *and* SUSAN *exit into the house*]

ROCKY What?
BINNIE I just wanna finish this.
ROCKY Aw, leave it alone.
BINNIE I can't. I just keep thinking about it. We made this solemn pact, right? We were both entitled to our secrets, we were never gonna spy on each other, we would always have our privacy. And then you leave your stuff at my place for one lousy night, and there I

go digging around like a—like a wife.

ROCKY I really wish you would leave this alone. [*aside*] I really do.

BINNIE But then I ask you to forgive me, and you just say, 'I forgive you,' like that. Rocky, if you did that to me, I wouldn't be here tonight! I'd still be so mad at you!

ROCKY So I'm a forgiving guy, okay? What's the problem?

BINNIE I just feel awful about it.

ROCKY *Look!* If it ain't broke, don't *fix* it, all *right?*

BINNIE Aw, now you're getting mad at me—

ROCKY Well, that's what you wanted, isn't it?

HEATHER [*enters from house*] Well, hi, kids. Anybody seen Greg?

ROCKY He was sittin' in the truck smokin' his face off.

HEATHER Typical. Well, Rocky, I'm glad you're here.

ROCKY Yeah. Well. Victor's party.

HEATHER I was so afraid you weren't coming. I hate that. See you two later. [*exit into house*]

BINNIE What was that all about?

[SUSAN, *without her coat and holding a soft drink, enters Tara's bedroom, looks around*]

ROCKY What're you askin' me for? Am I her translator'r something?

BINNIE Well, you seem to know what she's talking about.

ROCKY Binnie, you know me. I never know what anybody's talkin' about. Everybody else knows what they're all talkin' about except me. All right?

BINNIE All right.

ROCKY All right! Now let's go in an' enjoy this terrific freakin' party! [*exit into house*]

BINNIE [*to audience*] He's right. I shouldn't ask, if I don't wanna know. [*exit into house*]

[*Music up: current Top-Forty rock*]

Bedroom

Enter VICTOR

SUSAN Hi. Sorry. Didn't mean to snoop around. Just wanted to be alone for a minute. Gear up for this thing. [*aside*] He must think I'm such a flake.
VICTOR That's all right. You want me to leave?
SUSAN No! No. This is your sister Tara's room, right?
VICTOR Yeah. That's right, I forgot you've met her.
SUSAN Seems really nice to have, like, a normal family like you guys. Mom, Dad, Buddy and Sis. It's so unusual.
VICTOR Really?
SUSAN Yeah, well, I been living with my father. But then last year he got married again, and his new young airhead wife decided she didn't want me around, and the feeling was mutual, so I moved in with my mother and her husband. But now they've broken up, and my mother can't cope with having me around on top of her other problems.
VICTOR [*aside*] How could anybody not want her around?
SUSAN So anyway, I'm moving back to my father's and try to hack it with the Wicked Step-Bimbo. I don't know why I'm unloading this on you. I know it's really boring.

VICTOR No! Not at all! [*aside*] She's telling me her deepest secrets!
SUSAN Your sister's got a neat room.
VICTOR Yeah, she used to be a slob but she's grown up a bit.
SUSAN No, I meant—never mind. [*picks up bullhorn, speaks through it*] What's this for?
VICTOR Cheerleading. The kid is Captain of Grade Seven Cheerleading.
SUSAN Hey, the kid's growing up. And she's into guys, eh?
VICTOR Hey, the kid is twelve.
SUSAN [*aside*] I believe I will sit on the bed now. [*sits*]
VICTOR [*aside*] She sat on the bed. [*in*] I think it'd be kind of neat to have two houses to go to. You can't stand one parent, you just flake off to the other.
SUSAN It's horrible. It's all the family secrets. Every time I go to one house, they tell me secrets I'm not allowed to tell the other one. But then they bug me to tell them the other parent's secrets. I'm a double agent. It's the pits. [*aside*] Why am I telling him all this?
VICTOR [*aside*] This is great. She's telling me everything. [*in*] Sounds like the pits. [*aside, as he sits on the bed*] I am sitting on the bed.
SUSAN [*aside*] He's sitting on the bed. [*in*] I hate secrets. They always give me this sick guilty feeling. Whether I keep them or tell them.
VICTOR Tell you what. I want to make you a promise. I will never ask you to keep a secret for me. And I will never ask you to tell me a secret. [*aside*] Oh, why not go for it— [*in*] Even if tonight is the beginning of the greatest, maddest, most passionate love affair in history. [*aside*] Actually, this sounds kind of stupid, now that I, uh—

SECRETS

SUSAN Really? You mean that?
VICTOR [*aside*] She likes it! [*in*] Yes, really! I want you to have stuff I'll never find out. I want you to feel free with me. So to speak.
SUSAN [*aside*] He's not such a weird guy, really. And he *is* sort of attractive in his own unique way. [*she sits a little closer to him on the bed*]
VICTOR [*stretches, lets an arm drop across her shoulders. aside*] I'm putting my arm around her.
SUSAN [*aside*] And I'm letting him.
VICTOR [*aside*] And what do I do now? Don't answer that.
SUSAN [*aside*] I don't know why I'm letting him. He just made it perfectly clear he's as much of a horn-dog as the rest of them. Which means he's due to start climbing all over me any second now.
VICTOR [*aside*] At this point most guys would probably start to— I gotta come up with something nobody else would think of.
SUSAN [*aside*] But that thing about secrets is really nice.

[*A new rock song comes up, fast and raucous, in four-four time*]

VICTOR [*aside*] Got it. [*in*] Susan? May I have this waltz?
SUSAN What? Waltz?
VICTOR Please. [*stands, holds out hand*]
SUSAN You can't waltz to this!
VICTOR You ever try?
SUSAN No.
VICTOR How do you know till you try?
SUSAN [*aside*] He's different, I'll give him that. [*stands. In*] Okay. Let's try.

VICTOR That's the spirit.

[*They waltz to the rock music*]

[*aside*] This is great! What an inspired gimmick!

[*They continue waltzing*]

Porch

BINNIE [*enters from the house*] Worst party ever invented. Rocky's off brooding by himself because of this stupid fight over his bag. An' there's nobody else here worth talkin' to except Victor an' Susan, an' I don't know where they've got to. An' so I'm sitting by myself. An' wondering about that bloody note. I can't be sure. And that is such a weird feeling. I've never not been sure about Rocky before. This just doesn't feel like us. It feels like we're both somebody else.

CALVIN [*enters*] Hey, Bin.

BINNIE Hi.

CALVIN You're not gonna believe this. Susan went into one of the bedrooms, an' Victor went in after her, and they haven't been seen since.

BINNIE Really? That's great. So the party isn't a total loss.

CALVIN Well, it's a total loss to me.

BINNIE Why? You got the hot date from La La Land.

CALVIN Ah, she's more interested in Rocky than me.

BINNIE In Rocky?

CALVIN Oh, sure. Haven't you noticed? Rocky's always— uh, girls are always interested in Rocky.

SECRETS

BINNIE Well, of course I've noticed. [*aside*] No, I never noticed. Maybe it doesn't happen when I'm around. Maybe there's lots that doesn't happen when I'm around. [*in*] Actually, I know all about Rocky's girls. We got no secrets about that.
CALVIN No kidding.
BINNIE [*aside*] So there is something to know. [*in*] Oh, yeah, Rocky an' I have a, you know—an agreement.
CALVIN Oh, really? An—agreement? Well—listen, you're lookin' real good tonight.
BINNIE Thanks. [*aside*] Yuck. [*in*] Yeah, I know about Rocky an' Brooke, and, um—Rocky and Heather—
CALVIN Well, everybody knows about Rocky and Heather.
BINNIE [*aside*] Oh, no.
CALVIN Listen, you wanna dance?
BINNIE [*aside*] Oh, my God. [*in*] And Rocky and Anne—
CALVIN Rocky and Anne? Jeez, I didn't know *that*.
BINNIE Oh. Okay.
CALVIN I just know about Heather, and Mavis, and Andrea, and Jo-Anne, and you, of course …
BINNIE Of course. [*aside*] Oh, God. It can't be. Maybe he's just putting me on. Maybe it's like Susan, where everybody thinks it but it isn't true. [*in*] Yeah, well, he gets around.
CALVIN So, uh—you get around a bit too, do you?
BINNIE You might say that. [*aside*] Wait a minute, I've seen them! I've seen him talking with girls, and they'll see me, and they'll go, 'Hi, Bin'—and there's something in their faces. And I never noticed. They must think I'm such a pushover. And they're right, I am. I can't stand it.

CALVIN Wanna come in an' dance?
BINNIE Oh, why the hell not.
CALVIN [*wraps an arm around her*] Hey, baby, let's party!

[*They exit into the house*]

Bedroom

VICTOR *and* SUSAN *are still waltzing. Each of these asides is over the other person's shoulder, as they turn in the dance*

SUSAN [*aside*] This is so nice ...
VICTOR [*aside*] Maybe I should make my move on her.
SUSAN [*aside*] This is, like, *charming*.
VICTOR [*aside*] Course, if I try to kiss her, and she doesn't want me to kiss her, I'll ruin it.
SUSAN [*aside*] Romantic, almost—doing this stupid dance to the wrong music—and not having to worry about whether he's gonna hit on me.
VICTOR [*aside*] On the other hand, if she wants me to make a move on her, and I *don't* make a move on her, then she'll think I'm a *wuss*.
SUSAN [*aside*] So maybe this is what it's like with a man. A grownup. Somebody romantic and safe and interesting. I could get used to that.
VICTOR [*aside*] What the hey, go for it.

[*He kisses her, suddenly and clumsily. She pushes him off*]

SUSAN [*in*] All right, Swordfish, take it easy! [*aside*] Damn!

SECRETS

VICTOR Sorry. [*aside*] Damn!
SUSAN Let's not get carried away here, all right?
VICTOR I know. I'm sorry. [*aside*] Blew it!
SUSAN We agreed on what this date was gonna be about, so let's just stick to that, shall we?
VICTOR Yes Ma'am.
SUSAN I mean, look—I do like you, Victor—
VICTOR [*aside*] She likes me.
SUSAN I mean I don't know you that well, but you been a good friend to Binnie and I've always thought you were okay.
VICTOR [*aside*] She likes me.
SUSAN And I got no problem with you using me to tell them you're straight—
VICTOR I am not using you!
SUSAN Yes you are, Victor, it's fine, you're using me an' I'm using you.
VICTOR You are?
SUSAN Yeah, I didn't want to come to this party alone, 'cause there's people here I don't want to deal with, so you're my protector.
VICTOR [*aside*] Her protector? Sounds so manly.
SUSAN I don't mind being used. I'm used to it. I don't mind, as long as I'm in on it. But just—don't play games with this, all right? This does not mean I'm suddenly all available here.
VICTOR I know! I didn't think that! Look. I've obviously screwed up this date beyond redemption, so I might as well just tell you what's going on here—
SUSAN I know what's going on, Victor. You wanna stop the rumours, and you want a little action.
VICTOR No! I swear! Sure, some of it was to stop the

rumours. But that's an extra. The main thing— Oh, this is gonna sound so stupid.

SUSAN Why stop now? Sorry. Sorry. What?

VICTOR You're right, okay, I'll sound stupid. The main thing was this idiot fantasy that this might turn into a longer-term thing. I know, we've never even been that friendly! But the fact is, I'm really quite nuts about you. I like you an absolutely humongous amount, Susan.

And this business just now, sorry about that, but I don't date much, and I was just trying to show you— well, getting kind of—hoping maybe—I know, dumb dumb dumb dumb dumb—but I wasn't expecting anything. I swear, Susan, I was not thinking, like, 'Hey, here we go.' I've never believed any of those stories.

SUSAN No?

VICTOR Of course not! 'Cause look how they talk about me! An' none of *that's* true. And you know something? The look on their face when they tell those stories about you? It's exactly the same look when they make those jokes about me. So I know it's just locker-room garbage.

SUSAN Oh.

VICTOR I apologize for trying to kiss you.

SUSAN Apology accepted.

VICTOR Thank you. So look, let's get out of here, and you can go party with the others if you want, or I'll call you a cab and you can go home if you want—whatever you would like. What would you like, Susan?

SUSAN I would like to waltz, Victor.

[*And this time the music is actually a waltz. They waltz some more. The door opens and* CALVIN *bursts in*]

SECRETS

CALVIN Whoops! Victor, you got a second bathroom?
VICTOR Upstairs.
CALVIN Sorry if I interrupted anything, heh, heh. [*exit*]
SUSAN [*aside*] Oh, great.
VICTOR [*aside, not sarcastic*] Oh, great! Perfect! On top of everything else, somebody saw us! [*in*] You want me to lock the door? There is a lock. [*aside*] Whoops. [*in*] I mean, just, you know, if we want a little, you know, privacy. [*aside*] Digging myself in deeper.
SUSAN No, let's leave it unlocked.
VICTOR Sure. Whatever you want.
SUSAN [*aside*] That has such a safe, warm sound to it ... [*in*] Whatever I want?
VICTOR Of course.
SUSAN Okay.

[*She kisses him. They neck*]

Porch

ROCKY [*enters from the house*] I dunno what Binnie thinks she's doing. Dancing with that incredible dweeb. His date doesn't seem to mind. She keeps smiling at me. Actually, there's three or four other girls here who keep smilin' at me too. The ones I've—you know.

I never wanted to be that kind of a guy, with lots of different girls. Other guys talk about all the girls that they wish they could, you know—and I think, hey. I'm living the life they wish they was living. But I feel like such a loser.

It's like they say, when a guy sleeps around, he's a big

macho stud, but when a girl does it she's just a slut. Well, I don't feel like no big macho stud. I feel like a slut.

BROOKE [*enters from house*] Here I am!

ROCKY So you are.

BROOKE Bring your chain?

ROCKY What?

BROOKE That big chain you were hauling around. Didja bring it along?

ROCKY Why would I bring it? This is a party.

BROOKE Yes, I know that, thanks.

ROCKY [*aside*] Oh. She's talking sexy. I hate when they do that. I dunno how. So usually I just let 'em jump me. It's easier than talking.

BROOKE My date's having a good time with your girlfriend.

ROCKY Who? Binnie?

BROOKE Of course. Who did you think?

ROCKY I don't know.

BROOKE How many do you have?

ROCKY How many what?

BROOKE Girls.

ROCKY Who knows?

BROOKE Can't count that high?

ROCKY [*aside*] All right, now. Does she mean I can't count that high 'cause there's too many? Or 'cause I'm too dumb? Or both?

BROOKE Well?

ROCKY [*smiles at her*] Gee, I musta lost count back in, oh, I dunno, Grade Seven.

BROOKE Oh, dear. Well. Your date and my date seem to be having a good time together.

SECRETS

ROCKY So why don't we, right?
BROOKE Want to dance?
ROCKY Why the hell not.

[*She takes his hand, and they exit into the house*]

Bedroom

SUSAN *and* VICTOR *come out of their clinch, rather breathless*

SUSAN [*aside*] Wow.
VICTOR [*aside*] Hope that was okay.
SUSAN [*aside*] You wouldn't know it to look at him, would you.
VICTOR [*aside*] She's being awfully quiet. [*in*] Are you okay?
SUSAN Never been better.
VICTOR Great. Me neither. I like you.
SUSAN I know. You said.
VICTOR Oh, yeah. Sorry.
SUSAN That's okay. I like you too.
VICTOR [*aside*] What a time to have to go. [*in*] Uh—will you excuse me a minute? I'll be back in a minute.
SUSAN [*aside*] What a time to have to go. [*in*] Sure.
VICTOR Okay. Right. I'll be back real soon. Don't go 'way.
SUSAN Oh, I won't.
VICTOR Good. [*aside*] Wow. [*exit*]

Porch

ROCKY [*enters*] So now she's stopped dancing with that moron, and she's sitting in a corner of the room pretending to neck with him. But all the time she keeps sneakin' these little glances at me. With that look that she gets instead of crying an' screaming. I never know how to play these kinds of games. Gimme two teams, a ball an' a scoreboard any day.

[*Enter* VICTOR]

Yo, it's the Boa Constrictor. How's your date goin'?
VICTOR Wonderful. Wonderful. Absolutely wonderful.
ROCKY Yeah, I hear you an' Susan are makin' out.
VICTOR Well, I wouldn't put it like—well, yeah.
ROCKY Congratulations. Ya got protection?
VICTOR Oh, don't you start this stuff about Susan.
ROCKY It has nothin' to do with the crap about Susan. It's with everybody. Gotta play safe, man.
VICTOR Look, it would be great, and who knows, maybe some day. But that's not what tonight is about, okay?
ROCKY Okay. Chill. I'm just sayin', would you rather have one an' not need it, or need one an' not have it?
VICTOR Oh. Yeah. Good point.
ROCKY You don't got none, do you?
VICTOR Well, I don't keep 'em in the house 'cause I don't want Tara or my mom finding them, and I didn't buy any today 'cause I didn't want Susan to think I was that kind of a guy, or to think that I think she's that kind of a girl—
ROCKY Hey! This is the nineties, Victor, this is life or death!
VICTOR Yeah, and if my mom found them, it would be.

SECRETS

ROCKY What about your ol' man? Does he have any?
VICTOR My father? What for?
ROCKY For makin' balloon animals, what do you think for? How can such a smart guy be such a feeb? Why don't you go look, just in case?
VICTOR Steal my father's condoms? Do you have any idea how Freudian that is?
ROCKY So you wanna borrow from me, is that it?
VICTOR Well, if you insist. Just in case.
ROCKY [*takes from pockets*] I got three. Here, take 'em.
VICTOR All of 'em? What about you?
ROCKY Don't need 'em any more. I'm quitting.
VICTOR You're *what?*
ROCKY Givin' up on women. Gonna be a monk. [*gives him the condoms*]
VICTOR We gotta talk about this, okay? Not right now, but soon, okay?
ROCKY Hey, man. Be good to her.
VICTOR I really don't think it's gonna happen tonight, Rocky.
ROCKY I didn't say that. I just said, be good to her.
VICTOR I will. Thanks. Later.

[VICTOR *exist to the house.* ROCKY *stays on the porch and broods*]

Bedroom

SUSAN *sits on the bed, reading a magazine. Enter* VICTOR

VICTOR Now, then, where were we?
SUSAN I forget.

VICTOR So soon?
SUSAN Remind me.
VICTOR Okay.

[*They begin necking.* **VICTOR** *realizes that he's still holding the condoms in his hand*]

VICTOR [*aside, over her shoulder*] Great. Forgot to put them in my pocket. That's how nervous I am. The trick is—to get them into my pocket—without her noticing … [*he tries to do so*]
SUSAN What are you doing back there? [*she finds the condoms*] Oh.
VICTOR [*aside*] Oh, no. [*in*] Look, please don't get the wrong idea.
SUSAN Wrong idea?
VICTOR I wasn't actually intending to use them. I just borrowed these from Rocky to impress him.
SUSAN What? Wait a minute.
VICTOR [*aside*] Braaapp! Wrong answer.
SUSAN You borrowed these, not in case we had sex, but just to make the other guys think we're having sex?
VICTOR Just Rocky.
SUSAN Oh, Victor. I was really starting to think you were different.
VICTOR I am!
SUSAN No, you're not. You're just one of the guys.
VICTOR [*aside*] A few hours ago, that was all I wanted.
SUSAN Look, jerk. I got no problem with you having these. But you lied. You said you invited me 'cause you like me, and if they notice you're straight, that's a bonus.
VICTOR That's right.

SECRETS

SUSAN No, Victor, it's obvious: this is just so they'll notice you're straight. And these guarantee they know you're straight, right? 'Cause they know you're with Susan. And everybody knows about Susan.

VICTOR It's not like that.

SUSAN I got a little story for you, Victor. And this is a secret *I* expect *you* to keep. One day last year I was joking around with a bunch of guys in the caf. Sex jokes, you know. And somebody, I don't even remember who, made a crack about how he and I'd had a fling. The kind of joke that if he's lucky maybe they'll believe it. And I went along with it. Pretended it was true. I don't know why. Just to be outrageous.

And by that weekend, all the guys were telling each other stories about sleeping with Susan! It was amazing. Like wildfire. And I've never denied any of it. And I'll bet each one of those guys is convinced that everybody's had me except him. So here I am with the biggest reputation in the school—and I'm a virgin, Victor. What do you think of that?

VICTOR Why don't you tell them the truth?

SUSAN Who cares? Hell with 'em. If that's what they want, let them lie to each other. So this whole image, all tough and sexual, it's just a front. I'm like this outside, because inside I am scared spitless of other people. I pretend nothing bothers me, I'm not afraid of anything—and inside I feel like everybody's fine except me.

VICTOR But that's exactly how I feel. I'm scared too. Course, I'm not a virgin, but— [*aside*] Oh, who am I kidding? [*in*] All right, yeah. Me too, Susan. I've never done it either.

SUSAN Nothin' to be ashamed of.

VICTOR Easy for you to say. And that's a secret, by the way. I don't want that getting out, I got enough problems right now.
SUSAN Excuse me? What happened to that eternal vow you made about twenty minutes ago?
VICTOR Oh, God, you're right. I am such a mess!
SUSAN Well, I'll tell you what I'm gonna do. I am gonna go out there and spread the word all over this party—
VICTOR No! Please!
SUSAN That you and I have just been having major, passionate sex in here.
VICTOR What?
SUSAN I'm helping you out, Victor. Obviously that's what you want more than a relationship with me, more than anything. And it's no skin off my nose. So I'm gonna go tell everybody you're the great lover you want them to think you are—and then I'm going home.
VICTOR Susan, wait! Don't!

[*But she exits, leaving* **VICTOR** *sitting on the bed, miserable*]

Porch

BINNIE [*enters from house*] Okay, let's talk.
ROCKY Okay, what do we got to talk about? [*aside*] This is it.
BINNIE Let's talk about Heather. And Mavis, and Andrea, and Jo-Anne—
ROCKY [*aside*] Yeah, this is it. [*in*] What about 'em?
BINNIE Just tell me the truth, Rocky. Did you?

[*Pause, as* **ROCKY** *tries to frame an answer*]

SECRETS

BINNIE Never mind. Don't bother. Don't bother lying, don't even bother telling me the truth. How *could* you!
ROCKY I dunno.
BINNIE How long's this been happening?
ROCKY It hasn't been happening. It's over. It happened, like, once or twice.
BINNIE Once or twice? Once or twice *each*?
ROCKY It didn't mean nothin'! I don't even like them!
BINNIE *What?*
ROCKY You're the only one I care about. They're all a buncha slags.
BINNIE You absolute creep. It's bad enough you sleep with these girls, and lie to me about it—but then you have the absolute stones to *insult* them? To my *face*? What do you say about me, behind my back! Why do you *do* this, Rocky!
ROCKY I don't know! Why does a guy! To see if I can! To see what it's like! 'Cause it's there!
BINNIE I'm here too, Rocky.
ROCKY I know.
SUSAN [*enters*] Hey, guys, congratulate me. Me and Victor.
BINNIE Really? You're an item?
SUSAN Oh, yeah, I been going around the party telling everybody. It was great.
ROCKY Victor was great?
SUSAN Something wrong?
ROCKY No, nothing's wrong. Everything's perfect. I'm gonna get another drink. See you girls later. [*exit into house*]
SUSAN What?
BINNIE We're breaking up.
SUSAN What? You and Rocky?

Laura Myers (SUSAN) and Ruth McIntosh (BINNIE)

SECRETS

BINNIE Did you know this? Did you know he's had half the girls in the school?
SUSAN [*aside*] Oh, boy. [*in*] You're kidding.
BINNIE That note in his bag is just the tip of the avalanche. You never heard about this?
SUSAN Well—you hear all kinds of weird stuff—
BINNIE Susan! You heard something and you never told me?
SUSAN I didn't believe it!
BINNIE So? You could still tell me! What're you, protecting him? Thanks a lot! Best friend!

[BINNIE *turns her back, maybe cries.* SUSAN *stands watching her helplessly*]

Bedroom

ROCKY *comes in to find* VICTOR *sitting on the bed*

ROCKY Hey, man, you and Susan's all over the party.
VICTOR Oh, yeah? Great.
ROCKY Yeah, great. Looks like you're not homosexual no more.
VICTOR Amazing how that happens. How're you and Binnie doing?
ROCKY Great!
VICTOR Great. So. We're both doing great.
ROCKY So listen, I'll see you later, man. Take it easy.

[*He leaves*]

200

Porch / Bedroom

SUSAN I'm really sorry, Bin.
BINNIE I know. It's not your fault. And I'm glad to hear about you two, anyway. Nice to see something happening around here that isn't all lies.
SUSAN Uh, well, actually—
BINNIE What? You mean you didn't? You been lying?
SUSAN No. We didn't. I been lying. We talked. We danced. We made out a little. That was all.

[*In the bedroom,* VICTOR *stands, picks up the bullhorn*]

BINNIE Susan, you are weird. When *they* don't tell stories about you, *you* do!
SUSAN 'Cause that's all they want, Binnie. They don't want me.
BINNIE Are you nuts? Victor doesn't want you? Susan, the guy is smitten with you.
SUSAN Really?
BINNIE He is stricken!
SUSAN What's he said?
BINNIE *Said?* Look. If we're gonna learn anything from this god-awful night, it's forget what they *say*. It's the look in his eyes. You should see the look when you walk by.
SUSAN I saw that look tonight.
BINNIE Well, there you are, kid. Wake up and smell the caffeine.
ROCKY [*enters*] We gotta talk about this. Susan—excuse me, but we gotta talk about this.
SUSAN So talk.
BINNIE Yeah, go ahead. Talk.

SECRETS

VICTOR [*in bedroom doorway, talking through bullhorn*] I have an announcement. Your attention, please, everyone. I have an announcement.

[*Music cuts out*]

ROCKY What, he's gonna announce it now?
VICTOR There is a rumour going around this party that Susan and I are having a—relationship. We are not having a relationship. It's not true. It never happened.
ROCKY What?
VICTOR Repeat: Nothing has happened between Victor and Susan.
SUSAN Well, isn't that interesting.
VICTOR Also I am not gay. But I believe homosexuals are just as good as anybody else. So if certain infantile people need to feel more secure by deciding that means I am gay, that is their problem and not mine. Thank you. That is all. Resume partying.

[VICTOR *goes back into the bedroom. Music resumes*]

ROCKY Funny, usually it's the other way around, eh?
SUSAN How do you mean?
ROCKY Well, you know, the guy says they're having sex and the girl says they're not.
SUSAN Yeah, funny about that.
ROCKY So which of you is—uh—
SUSAN Lying?
ROCKY I was gonna say, telling the truth.
SUSAN That's a much nicer way of putting it, Rocky.

See you guys later. [*to* BINNIE] Holler if you need anything. [*exit to house*]

BINNIE [*aside*] Sure, I need my boyfriend back.

ROCKY Awright, I'll tell you what's going on. I've always wanted you to be happy. So I've always gone along with stuff the way you wanted it. I mean, we never really agreed not to see other people, did we. You just started saying this was how it was gonna be. An' I never said nothin'. I never felt like it was the right time when—

BINNIE Oh, shut up.

ROCKY What?

BINNIE What part of 'shut up' don't you understand? Cut the crap. Stuff a sock in it. Squelch yourself. You understand that?

ROCKY I'm just sayin', if you wanna keep goin', we can keep goin'. Like we have been.

BINNIE You mean with you running around on me? [*aside*] I'm gonna lose him. Right now.

ROCKY It doesn't have to be like that. We can be honest with each other. I just don't know if we should be, you know, one-on-one alla time.

BINNIE No. You have to be all mine, or we got nothing. [*aside*] That's it. I just lost him.

ROCKY Binnie, I care about you just as much as ever.

BINNIE Sorry, Rocky, I need more than that. [*starts to exit to the street*] I'll see you around.

ROCKY Wait a minute! We can still be friends, right? Like we always were!

BINNIE Rocky. We weren't friends. You were friends. Just like you're friends with all of them. I was never 'friends.'

[ROCKY *exits to the street. She watches him go*]

[*to audience*] I'll be damned. I thought I was losing him. I didn't lose him. I freakin' well *dumped* him. [*exit the other way*]

Bedroom

Enter VICTOR *and* SUSAN

SUSAN That was interesting.
VICTOR I don't care what they think of me any more.
SUSAN How about what they think of me?
VICTOR I was trying to help with that.
SUSAN By making me look like a liar?
VICTOR Well, sorry, Susan, but you were a liar. You said we did stuff we didn't do. I just didn't want you to look like—um—
SUSAN Like a slut.
VICTOR No, that's not what I was—
SUSAN So instead, you made me look so desperate for love that I make it up when it's not true.
VICTOR You mean like me.
SUSAN [*pause*] I didn't mean that.
VICTOR Tell you what. I'll tell them I begged you to say we were doing it. And you agreed, out of pity for me. How's that?
SUSAN You think they're gonna believe I'm such a sucker?
VICTOR Aren't you?

[*Pause. They look at each other, amused, with some returning affection*]

SUSAN [*stands, takes his hand*] I will not let you go out there and tell them what losers we both are. We will both go out there, together, holding hands if you like—hey, who knows, maybe we'll even dance. And let the cretins think whatever they want. C'mon.

[*She starts to go.* VICTOR *holds back*]

What?
VICTOR Well, as long as you realize they're gonna keep on thinking we're a couple. An item. And, you know, all that that entails.
SUSAN So?
VICTOR So it's not true.
SUSAN Not quite. But you gotta start somewhere.

[*She kisses him. They look to the audience. One or both seems about to deliver an aside. Then they decide the hell with it, smile, and exit together, holding hands*]

Editor for the Press: Robert Wallace
Cover Design: Clare McGoldrick / Reactor
Photographs: David Cooper
Printed in Canada

COACH HOUSE PRESS
50 Prince Arthur Avenue
Suite 107
Toronto, Canada
M5R 1B5